ENRICO ACERBI

ALL ABOUT AUSTERLITZ

The campaign, the battle, the places and the troops

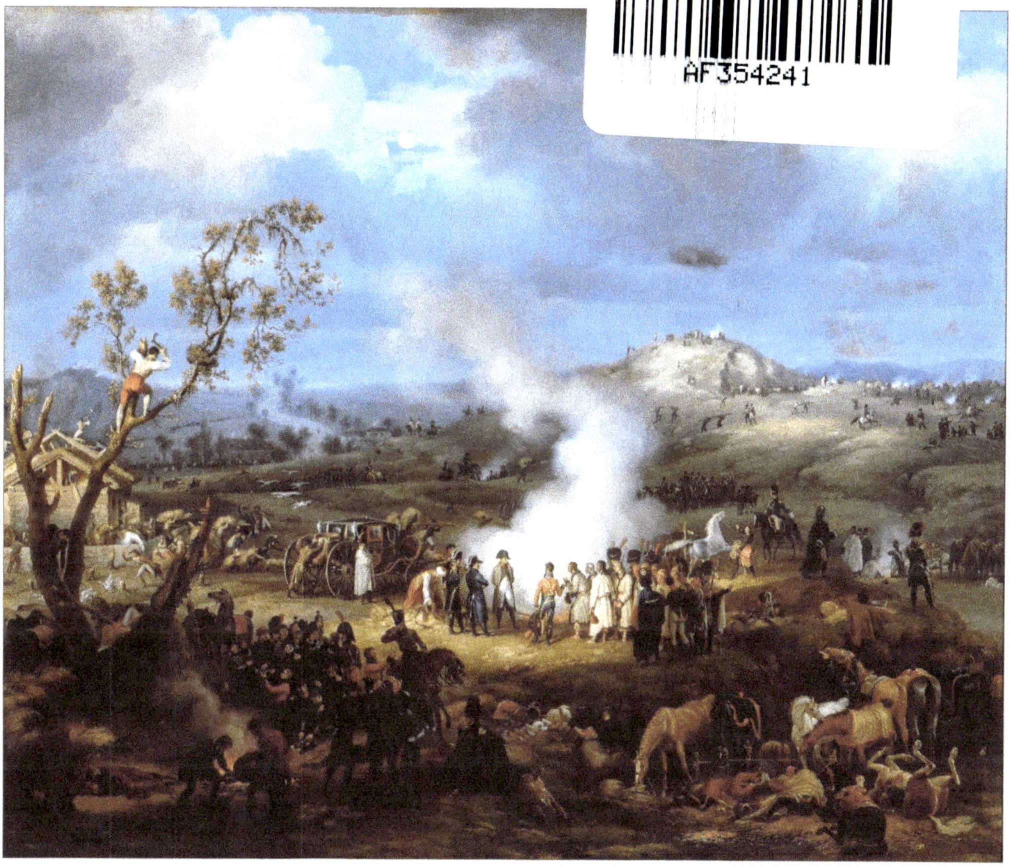

BATTLEFIELD 027

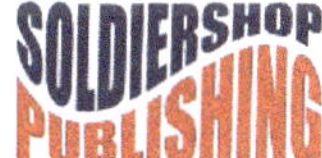

AUTHOR

Enrico Acerbi was born in Valdagno (Vicenza) on 13.8.1952; graduated in medicine, expert in toxicology, worked in the local hospital, now retired. Partner of the War Museum of Rovereto, member of the Napoleonic Association of Italy and historiographer of the Great War. Enrico Acerbi has developed a passion for historical research since the 1990s. For five years he collaborated with the Center for Great War Studies in Asiago. He has also collaborated with the Comunità Montana of Arsiero as a teacher at the popular university (historical training courses on the First World War) and with the Comunità Montana of Agno-Chiampo (reconstruction of the fortifications made during the Great War). Partner of the War Museum of Rovereto and founding member of the Historical Research Group on the Great War of Valdagno, currently engaged in the study of Napoleonic history in Veneto and Italy. Graphic illustrator of articles on Napoleonic history. He has to his credit several historical publications for various publishers and several titles also for Soldiershop!

EDITORIAL NOTES

LICENSES COMMONS

▲ Capture of the eagle of a French regiment by the Russian Guard, by Bogdan Willewalde

ISBN: 9788893278614 1st edition May 2022
ALL ABOUT AUSTERLITZ
Text and image by Enrico Acerbi. Color uniform plates cured by Luca Cristini and Nadir Durand
Publisher: Luca Cristini Editore per i tipi di Soldiershop. Cover & Art Design: Luca S. Cristini.

The Battle of Austerlitz
Testimonies and guide to the alignments

INTRODUCTION: AUSTERLITZ AGAIN?

Yes, Austerlitz again. Everything has been said and told about that famous battle of December 2, 1805, which represents one of the high points of Bonaparte's "genius". The battle of Austerlitz has been emphasized as the battle of the Three Emperors, the last of whom, considered in Europe as a "parvenu" was Napoleon himself. It was one of the battles that had the honor of giving its name to one of the most important railway stations in Paris, Gare de Austerlitz, as well as giving its name to a bridge over the Seine, opened in 1807, iron and toll. These banal considerations are evidence of how the new emperor was pleased with the campaign of 1805 and its final outcome.

Given the importance of the event, we can testify how, on the battle, has been written in massive measure in the world, especially in the Anglo-Saxon, fascinated by the clash and the legends related to it, we can also underline how, on Austerlitz, was made a small masterpiece film by Abel Gance. The very beautiful film also carries with it some curiosities: in the scene where you see the British Prime Minister William Pitt, in his London office, around the beginning of 1800, if you look out the window you can see the Houses of Parliament and Big Ben more than 60 years before they were built.

A lot has already been written, but not much in Italian, except for the fluent volume of Sergio Valzania, (*Austerlitz. Napoleon's greatest victory*, Mondadori 2017), which is a pleasure to read even if, in my opinion, the title is already out of tune; Austerlitz was a great gamble, but calling it Napoleon's greatest victory seems a bit reductive compared to other battles such as Rivoli and Marengo. In this sense, therefore, I wanted to bring my contribution to how that battle was faced and judged, overcoming stereotypes such as "the fog" and the famous "Austerlitz sun", using sources of different nationalities and inserting, where possible, some direct testimony of combatants.

The battle theater is located in the Czech Republic, near Brno (the Habsburg Brünn). Those who visit the battle sites, those who go there for a historical reenactment, may be interested to know what was the exact deployment of the troops and what remains to be seen today in those places. I did not want to make a guide to the battlefield (there are already some) but only to give some clues to make less heavy the narration of the deployments, trying to detail them as much as possible.

The Battle of Austerlitz was not a one-off battle, but a drama in three acts, full of individual confrontations, some of them atypical and bloody, such as the great cavalry charge. There was a halting battle in the north that was essentially to keep the French Reserves pinned down (according to the Allies) or mask the decisive attack in the central part, which remained poorly defended (according to Napoleon).

In the south there was the Allied attack in force, which was supposed to upset the French flank and make it give way (according to the Austrian Chief of Staff Weyrother) and which came very close to achieving its objective, so much so that it was feared that Napoleon himself would end up being a victim of its trap. Among other things, Weyrother, did nothing more than replicate, in force, what he himself had drawn up, as a plan of attack, at Rivoli in 1797: at the time the attack on the French wing was designed for a single attacking column, while at Austerlitz there were at least three, and very strong.

At the center of the battle was decided, thanks to Soult's attack on Pratzen, which ended up cutting the enemy army in two; an attack finely timed and calculated by the skilled reasoner that was the Empereur. It was a beautiful victory, prepared since the days that preceded it, in a crescendo of episodes, some similar to pieces of a play.

Austerlitz, even today, has a remarkable charm. The historical reenactment of the battle, in 2021, was cancelled for health safety reasons, and the 2020 reenactment progressed in a subdued fashion, again for health safety reasons. In 2018, however, the last grand reenactment saw the reenactment of the battle under Santon Hill, with about 1,000 uniformed figures, 60 horses and 15 cannons, and another simulated clash at the Peace Monument.

I hope that this small volume on the battle can offer some insights and answer to some curiosity, without having the pretension to place side by side works of much more solid consistency.

▲ Photo of the Austerlitz field with reenactors in French uniforms. Courtesy by Keith Redfern

THE "SEVEN TORRENTS" AND A *GRANDE ARMÉE*

Austerlitz is a victory for Napoleon, one of the most brilliant of his career and should be understood starting from afar: on the banks of the English Channel where the French army was in training waiting to invade England and where comes the news of the formation of yet another anti-French coalition: the third.

The Field of Boulogne. In the 19th century, England was a great economic and political power and opposed to France's expansion projects. In 1803, Napoleon decided to organize a large military camp in order to invade England. It is a considerable challenge. He chose the port of Boulogne, on the English Channel, to install the camp, which could accommodate from 150,000 to 200,000 soldiers. Important work was done to dig the basins for the ships, and to build barracks for the troops with new roads for circulation. The regiments were trained to embark and disembark in good order, as quickly as possible. On August 16, 1804, Napoleon visits the fields of Boulogne for a collective ceremony to award the newly created Legion of Honor. A crowd of 100,000 men attend the ceremony that will last more than seven hours. The project of the invasion of England is abandoned in August 1805, as Austria is allying with Russia to enter the war: Napoleon launches his Grande Armée on the field.

The army of the invasion, which, later, Napoleon will officially call *"Grande Armée"*, is organized in seven **ARMY CORPS** (or Corps, which will be defined later as *"les sept torrents"*, seven torrents that flowed on the roads) commanded by Marshals Bernadotte, Davout, Soult, Lannes, Ney, Au-

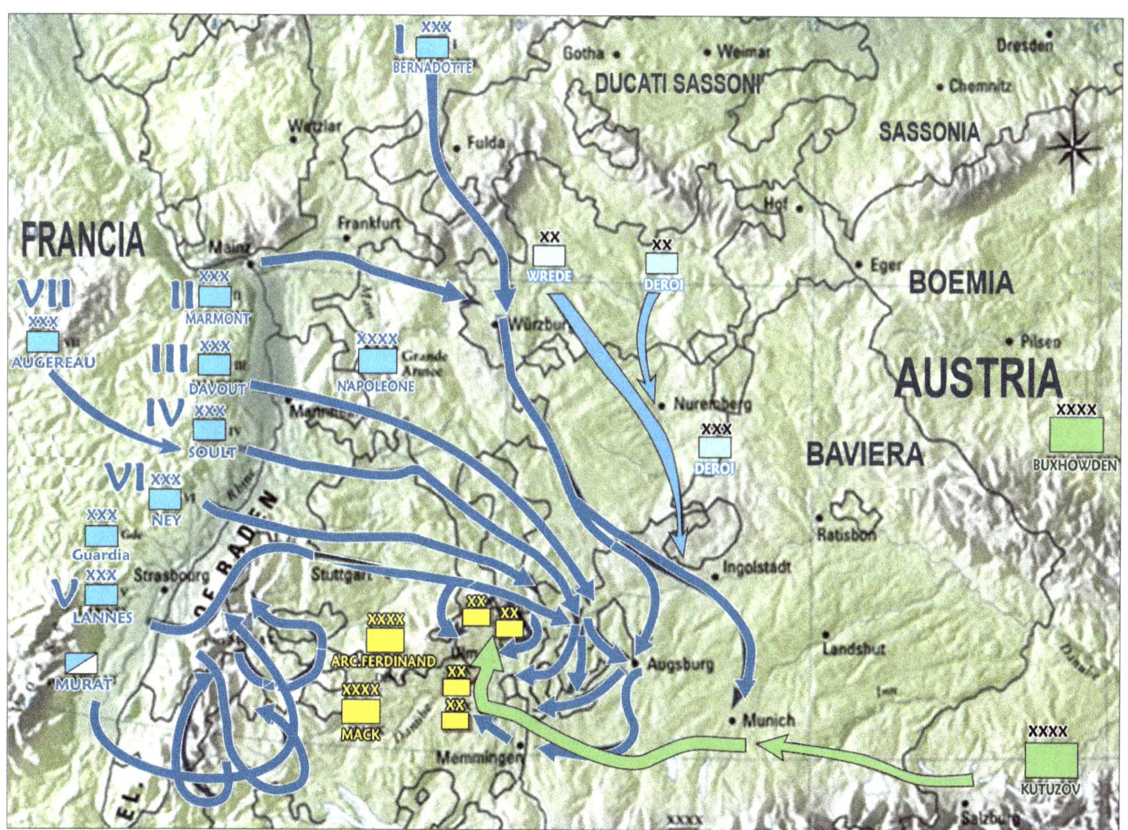

gereau and Marmont. The Corps will make the 1805, 1806 and 1807 campaigns (on October 1, 1806 they will add an 8th Corps of Mortier and also a 9th composed of Bavarian, Badense and Wurtemburg allies - under Prince Jérôme Bonaparte; in 1807 the 10th Corps of Lefebvre will also make its appearance). The first Grande Armée, born precisely in 1805, will be disbanded in 1808. The Corps are defined as "Seven streams" because each one has its own route of march, which prevents it from impeding the movement of the others and supplies itself in sectors of territory, different for each corps; they march like long endless columns, like torrents in flood.

The corps are a creation of Napoleon Bonaparte in 1805, an idea originated from the memory of the three corps of the Armée de Réserve of 1800, right, central and left; however those, in 1800, were only troop groupings, without services, which remained the responsibility of the individual divisions.

The Emperor grouped the divisions into large units of infantry, cavalry and even artillery, creating sufficiently small and agile groups to be able to live off the resources of the occupied countries, thanks to the fact that they followed different routes, thus freeing themselves from complex logistics and allowing great mobility. The Corps, must march, separated from each other by only **one day's march**; therefore, in case of battle, they can also concentrate in a decisive point, very quickly and support each other.

Someone has already heard of the **Bataillon Carré**. In fact, it is the way of marching of the Corps that advance while remaining in support of each other, separated by not long distances (the name comes from a letter from Napoleon to Soult, dated October 5, 1806) The *Grande Armée* moved in an imaginary square (**carré**) of 50 km. The opposite mode of marching was represented by the **Marche Manoeuvre**.

In time, the French (and Prussian) Corps would become structured on the territory (territorial Army Corps including the Corps' own divisions) making it easier to manage the immediate availability of officers and making mobilization quick in case of war. The Russian and Austrian Corps, on the other hand, were and would remain units created extemporaneously at the beginning of the war.

For the first time in military history, an Army Corps brings together multiple divisions under a single command. They are seven small autonomous armies under the command of a Marshal. Their numbers in 1805, but will be constantly increasing under the Empire, are as follows: from 25000 to 30000 men (in 1812, in the Russian campaign, they will be about 81000 men each.

Army Corps of the *Grande Armée* 1805 --- The Corps was born from a logistical need to supply the territory, a small autonomous army and all following different routes, however, all are reachable, a day's march.

--- Each army corps includes a staff of about forty officers. Approximately 100 administrative staffs manage health, supplies, mail, and treasury.

--- The traditional artillery, engineer, and train logistical apparatus remains with the divisions at first.

--- the Corps has two or three infantry divisions with their artillery (two six-piece and one eight-piece batteries), a light cavalry division or brigade, and the train.

Gradually, though:

--- the divisions lose their cavalry. The corps may dispose of cavalry as scout and screen troops while awaiting the arrival of slow troops.

--- The divisions assign part of their artillery to the corps, which provides itself with a park of pieces and ammunition.

--- the divisions concur to form the corps Engineer.

Each corps has four to two divisions. The division, so called because it was a "slice" of an army, is the tactical unit for ec-cellency, created by Carnot at the time of the Revolution, commanded by a divisional general. It possessed about 5000-8000 men, as effective. Each division, prior to 1805, had its own infantry, artillery, genius, train, and cavalry. Each division corresponded to a similar territorial Lever Division. The 1805 Corps had infantry divisions with separate artillery and cavalry, but able to cooperate. The advantage of the corps over the division is that it is more indi-pendent and more autonomous. It is a reducing army - since it brings together all three arms - that moves quickly. It is usually easy to group Army Corps in a battlefield.

In addition to the Army Corps, there is the Imperial Guard, the Emperor's personal defense. It is commanded by four Marshals and is made up of elite troops. In 1805 it had 12000 men (in 1813 it will reach 81000 men). The Guard had its own regiments of infantry, cavalry, artillery, genius and train; from 1809 onwards, the Guard was also divided into Old, Medium and Young, according to the soldiers' battle experience and period of service. Four military campaigns are required to join the Guard since the Consular of 1800.

Soldiers are recruited by conscription: all young men between the ages of 20 and 25 must be ready to go to war and are drawn. To be recruited, a man must be healthy and without disabilities. The regiments bring together inexperienced young men and old soldiers who have served in several military campaigns. Soldiers learn in a few days to walk in step, obey orders, use weapons, and care for their equipment. Advancement is decided on the basis of experience (it takes 4 years of service between each rank to become a captain) and sometimes an act of arms or a heroic act is enough.

The cavalry is the spearhead of the *Grande Armée*. It is commanded by a Marshal with about 12000 men (32000 men and horses in 1813). It is divided into heavy cavalry or reserve (cuirassiers and carabiniers), line cavalry (dragoons) and light cavalry (hussars and chasseurs à cheval).

THE MORAVIAN TRAP

History (the one of the winners) has established that the battle of Austerlitz was lost because of an ill-considered plan drawn up by the Austrian Chief of Staff, Franz von Weyrother. Of course, we would be naive to believe that everything was reduced to the bad application of the Austro-Russian plan of attack, as if the French did not exist or were only extras. Napoleon too, of course, has a plan; his plan. In the case of 1805 or the Olmütz maneuver (as in the Friedland maneuver) Napoleon will operate in such a way as to force his opponent to make a mistake on the battlefield.

After the Austrian disaster of Ulm, with the almost total disappearance of the best imperial troops, the Russian general Kutuzov goes beyond the Inn and the Danube to try to rejoin the two approaching Russian armies: Buxhöwden and Bennigsen. Napoleon pursues, above all to avoid the possible union of the Allies with the Army of Italy of the two archdukes Carl and Johann.

The 29 October Kutuzov calls a council of war to Wels (in Austria, on the Traun) with the Emperor Franz II (title still of the Sacred Roman Empire). It is decided to take time to wait for the two archdukes, to join them in Sankt Polten, where it is planned to give battle taking advantage of the heights of the place. The French take, in the meantime, Braunau and make it their base of support. Their cavalry vanguard engages the retreating Allied troops at Ried and Lambach, but the Austrians escape by burning the bridges over the Traun. Kutuzov, fearing an outflanking by Murat's cavalry, has his first encounter with French cavalry (Amstetten) on November 5 and blocks it, allowing his troops to cross the Danube to the north four days later at Melk.

Napoleon's chasing comes into crisis due to an unexpected initiative of Murat, who, instead of guarding the left bank of the Danube, throws himself into the *glorious* conquest of Vienna. On the right bank of the river remains alone the new corps of Mortier, few troops without cover. Kutuzov takes advantage of the situation to devastate the unfortunate Mortier at Dürrenstein (Dürnstein). The Empereur thunders and strikes Murat, but forgives him by virtue of the armistice gained by occupying the Thabor bridge (the largest in Vienna). However, he sends him back to pursue without respite Kutuzov , who deploys his rearguard (Bagration) to Hollabrünn; there the Russians and the French clash on November 15. Bonaparte now resumes in hand the initiative of the campaign.

Here Murat combines another one of his; he adheres to Bagration's cease-fire request, thinking it would be good to wait to be joined by Lannes and Soult's infantry, but he does not realize that doing so allows Kutuzov to escape and move away again. On November 16, an angry message from Napoleon makes him understand the stupidity committed: *"I have no words to describe my irritation. You command only my vanguard and you have no right to make armistices without consulting me! You are making me lose the fruits of the whole campaign [...] The Austrians played games in the passage of the bridge of Vienna, you let yourself be beaten by the nose by an aide de camp!"*

The mortified Murat decidedly alternated his best with his worst. Desperate for redemption he immediately attacks Hollabrünn but meets fierce resistance. In the meantime, Kutuzov is repaired to Olmütz where he joins the 40.000 men of Buxhöwden (with the Tsar in person). Napoleon is now more than 700 km from his logistical bases in Vienna, with the prospect of facing an Allied army of 85,000 men.

Time favors the Austro-Russians, who can receive further reinforcements or even wait for the end of the Prussian doubts, whose neutrality is becoming weaker every day. Napoleon must act promptly and quickly. After having abandoned the tactics of the frantic pursuit, he takes a break, "lets his turn pass". By now he has understood that pursuing an old fox like Kutuzov is not only ineffective, but would take him further and further away from his logical bases, in the heart of a hostile Europe and under the possible threat of 150,000 mobilized Prussians. In his mind, *"the Austerlitz machination"* comes to the fore, the deception that will prove fatal to the refusing enemy. The French solution consisted in forcing the adversaries to resume the offensive on a front that allowed the Empereur to concentrate his forces in that sector, thanks to the use of the Bataillon Carré, obtaining a decisive victory. In fact, after having occupied Brno, on November 20, he will make frequent reconnaissance in the area of the ponds, about twenty kilometers away. He will tell his companions: *"Look well at this land! It will become a battlefield. Here you will have to play your part very well."*

> *"When, on November 17, the news spread that the French had entered Moravia, near Znajm (Znojmo) the people panicked. Those who could, managed to flee quickly, including the authorities and administration. The imperial road was jammed with carts and traffic, as in a modern rush hour. The road was permanently blocked and no public offices were in operation,"* says Jan Čupík of Olešnice, in his chronicle of the town. *"the town was evacuated on November 18 and abandoned by the soldiers of the garrison of the Špilberk fortress (Silvio Pellico's famous Spielberg). The inhabitants were seized by panic and terror; fear and anguish reigned. Those who were destined to stay were distraught and the bourgeoisie had to defend their possessions with their own strength. The first French, a company of chasseurs on horseback of Marshal Murat, together with other cavalry, entered Brno on Tuesday, November 19. They entered through the Brno Gate at the height of the present-day Pekařská Street and immediately broke through the city walls. The whole city was occupied within minutes. All that could be heard was the sound of horses' hooves pounding. Thus died the regular rhythm of the main Moravian and Silesian city. All the Cafes and Warehouses remained closed and it really looked like a dead city. One could only see, here and there, a few French soldiers."* This was the memory of the curate of Myslibořice for that November 19, 1805 in Brno.

L'Empereur imagines that a secret agreement between the Coalition and the Prussians plays against him. Tsar Alexander, in fact, managed to convince Frederick William III of Prussia to sign the agreement (November 3, 1805) at Postdam; according to the pact Prussia pledges to enter the war within a month if France refuses its conditions of "mediation". Its entry into the war would lead to the invasion of Bohemia with a strong army of about 150,000 men; a dramatic situation for Napoleon. Moreover, every day that passes, the possibility of Austro-Russian reinforcements increases: as suggested by Prince Czartoryski and Kutuzov himself, if the Coalition had retreated further east, it could have joined, in Hungary, the forces of Archdukes Johann and Carl, who were retreating in that direction at the head of another 80,000 men.

Napoleon established his headquarters on November 20 in Brünn, 65 km southwest of Olmütz; from there he staged a pantomime that would last several days. Suddenly he orders his cavalry to show timidity and to refuse any combat against the Austro-Russians; he sets a trap by deciding to make, on November 21, an advanced cavalry outpost, without infantry or cannon support, around the village of Wischau, halfway between Brünn (Brno) and Olmütz (Olomouc).

> "The French Emperor appeared in Brno dressed in a brown cloak and with the typical two-horned hat, by which he differed from his Marshals and Generals. He appeared at about 17 o'clock in the evening (the sun had set) and was accompanied by ma mysterians, who looked like demons, bare-chested, with their faces burned by the sun and ravaged by beards. Around their waists they had a wide band with knives and a short saber in the shape of a snake." recounts the curate Horký. "As a sign of celebration, Napoleon, ordered that each window have two lit candles. They shone like so many stars in the night. It was certainly not a sign of affection for that Emperor, but Napoleon's orders struck fear."

So, while the curates write down their anger in their notebooks, Treilhard's and Milhaud's vanguard cavalry brigades, which are positioned in Wischau, receive orders not to move more than two leagues (8 km) away from that village. Their only support were the dragoons of the Walther division, who were stationed at Murat's headquarters in Rausnitz (15 km east of Brünn and 5 km north of Austerlitz) with Margaron's *chasseurs à cheval* acting as liaison between Walther's dragoons and the infantry divisions Legrand, Saint-Hilaire and Vandamme. Lannes and the V Corps are further back between Brno, where the Guard is stationed, and Bellowitz. The bait soon attracts Russian cavalry. On November 25, a first attack repulses the French Hussars, soon supported by Walther's dragoons that restore order in the Wischau outpost. The partial success, however, excites the Tsar who, despite the advice of Kutuzov, aimed at preventing a commitment in battle to his tired troops, with the support of the Austrian Emperor, gives in to the sirens of the offensive. Thus a clash between opposing cavalries is ignited.

Kutuzov is overruled by the Tsar's favorite, the young prince Dolgoruki (and by the less young, 51 years old, Austrian chief of staff Franz von Weyrother). The plan to parade towards Hungary in search of reinforcements is rejected in favor of a new plan of attack. The Tsar, in fact, believes he can attack the Grande Armée that he thinks is dispersed and demoralized. The skirmish of November 25 only reinforced his thinking.

To comfort the idea materialized in the mind of the Russian Emperor, Napoleon sends him, on a mission, his aide-de-camp, General Savary, with a letter of congratulations that writes *"his ambition to earn your friendship"*.

We are in the presence of the diplomatic part of the "Moravian trap" and Napoleon wants to show himself on the defensive. Savary, an intelligence specialist (he is the direct superior of agent Schulmeister, recently appointed General Commissioner of Police in Vienna), takes advantage of this to collect information on the Austro-Russian force and its movements. Having arrived 4 km beyond Wischau, Savary crosses the Russian lines and is escorted to Olmütz. At 8 a.m. on November 26, he is received by the Czar as the Coalition troops appear to begin moving southwest. The Tsar reads the letter and responds in vague and dilatory terms. Upon his return Savary informs Napoleon of what he has observed, of the young officers surrounding the Czar, eager to "seize the laurel of glory against the revolutionary dragon." L'Empereur understands that the deception is working and sends Savary back to ask for an interview with the Tsar and, without waiting for the Russian response, puts

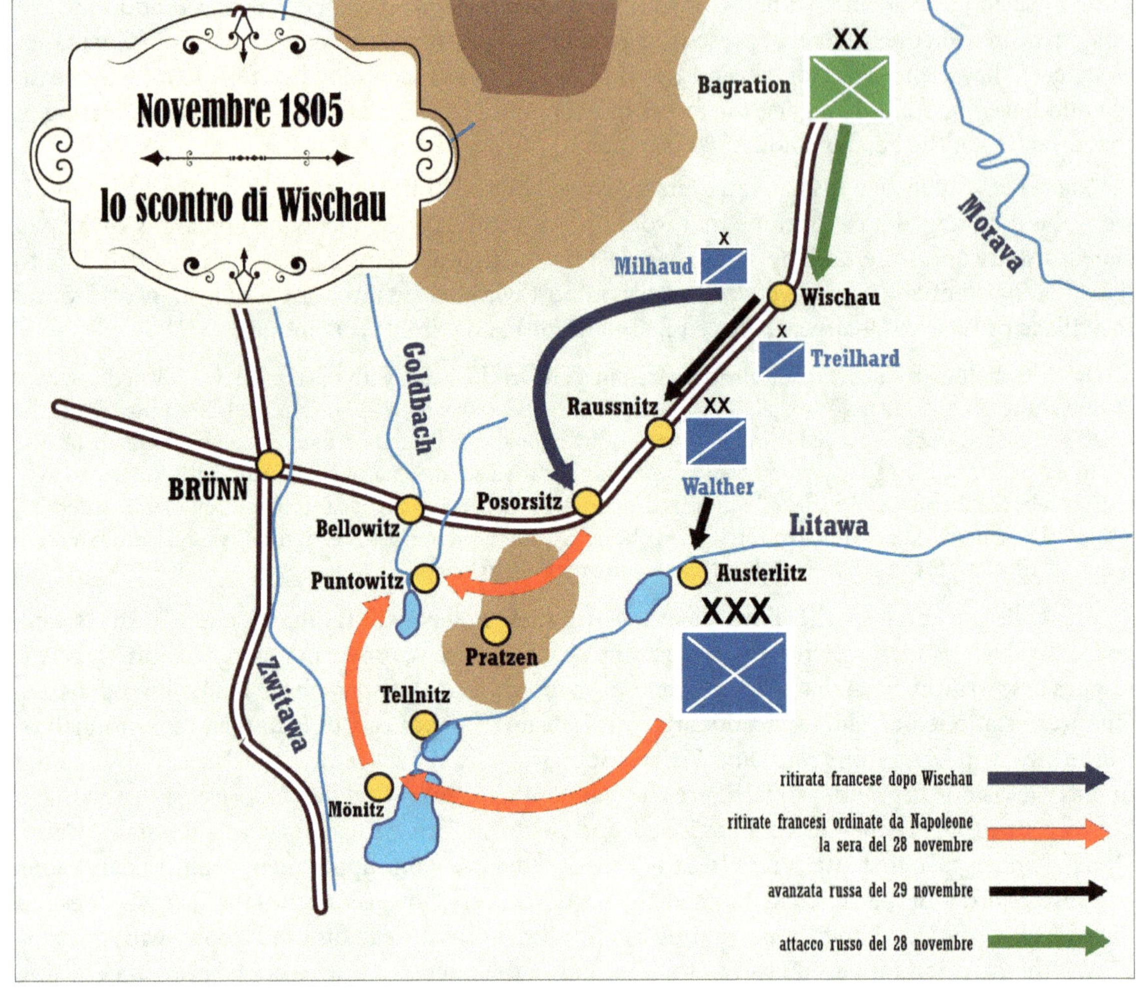

Davout on alert in Vienna. Bonaparte thinks he must wait at least 48 hours before starting a combat retreat to his own reinforcements.

In the meantime the Coalition army has moved. The vanguard is led by the hero of Hollabrünn, Prince Bagration, a Georgian (thanks to his fellow countryman Stalin, he will give his name to the northern part of Preussisch-Eylau). He advances on three columns: one on the road, the other two on the sides of the road in order to surround the position of Wischau. The Hussars of Treilhard, assisted by the Dragoons of Walther, hold out; however a retreat is necessary due to the arrival of about thirty Russian squadrons. Prince Dolgoruki, the one who wants glory in attack, leads the charge under the eyes of the Tsar, capturing a hundred Frenchmen. On the evening of November 28, the Russians occupy Wischau and Murat, set aside between Wischau and Raussnitz, withdraws to Posorsitz where he establishes his new Headquarters.

Napoleon's request for an interview arrives punctually to incite the Austro-Russians to resume the offensive. In fact the situation is even better than Bonaparte could imagine: the Coalition has already decided to attack the French right to block the road to Vienna. Alexander I has decided to bring to his left all the bodies that initially stood on his right during the march from Olmütz to Wischau. The precipitous French retreat from Wischau and Savary's demands changed the Czar's mind about the possibility of outflanking the opposing left wing to the north for easier maneuver on the enemy right.

Giving the impression that he feared a defeat, Napoleon accentuated his retreat operations by ordering a general retreat west of the Goldbach. Under cover of this retreat, in fact, the Empereur is already deploying his troops to battle. After a long inspection between Posorsitz and Holubitz, a little further south, on the evening of November 28 Bonaparte stops at the Old Post Office in Posorsitz where he writes his orders: Soult must evacuate the village of Austerlitz and fall back west of the Goldbach along the Littawa valley; Lannes' V Corps must remain on the road to Olmütz west of Bellowitz, with Murat's Guard and reserve cavalry nearby. Thus Napoleon can count on 58000 men against about 75000 Austro-Russians. Should they attack on the 29th, Napoleon must conduct a resistance battle, awaiting the arrival of Bernadotte's and Davout's corps, who have orders to aim for Brno.

"A curiosity. After the retreat of Kutuzov and the taking of the city by Napoleon's soldiers, Marshal Lannes took lodging in the building of the Vegetable Market in Brno. Unfortunately, from his window he did not have a good view. The Vegetable Market became at that time a huge bloody and smelly slaughterhouse. The French demanded a daily tribute of 26000 pounds of food from the city, which corresponded, more or less, to 23 cows. The peasants brought their cattle to the square, where the French slaughtered them on the spot. At that time, the attention for the hygienic norms was very poor, so the miasma and the smells of the slaughtered cattle penetrated almost all the city. To be precise, the local population had to give the occupants 5000 pairs of shoes and, every day, 26000 pounds of food (more or less 11.8 tons), 20000 loaves of bread and 14000 of had or hay. It must be said that this type of food requisitions in foreign territories was quite common at the time, even in other armies ".

On November 29 Savary sends a request for armistice negotiations, but this time Alexander refuses to receive it and instructs Prince Dolgoruki to represent him. For the Tsar it is clear that Napoleon does not want to fight. The evening of the 29th Dolgoruki meets the Empereur at the outposts near Posorsitz. That meeting, described by Savary, is the key to all the psychological strategies of the *"Moravian trap"*. In spite of Dolgoruki's arrogant tones, which made the French officers present at the interview quiver with indignation, Bonaparte calmly probed his interlocutor, who dished out the Coalition's demands: *"Yes to Peace if France abandons the right bank of the Rhine, Italy and Belgium and if, first, she abandons Vienna by returning behind the Danube, leaving Austria behind."*

After dismissing Dolgoruki and his insulting demands, Napoleon lets his anger explode by cracking his whip, but the act is successful. The Russian prince will report to the Czar that *"Napoleon was trembling with fright"* and that *"A vanguard was enough to beat him."* Goal achieved: the Austro-Russians had agreed to attack in battle.

After ordering Soult to evacuate Austerlitz and deploy west of the Goldbach stream, on November 30, Bonaparte wrote: *"If I wanted to prevent the enemy from outflanking my right, I would place myself on those fine heights (the Pratzen Ndt.) and have a regular battle with them; indeed I would have the advantage of position but ... if the enemy saw us so well deployed he could make no mistake."*

It is therefore the intent of the Empereur, having deceived his opponents, to force them to make fatal errors; he could not do this unless he abandoned the heights of Pratzen. In practice he will expose his unarmed flank, enticing the Austro-Russians to take advantage of it. The Grande Armée's retreat of November 29 provokes its immediate effects. The Coalition occupies Austerlitz that same evening, for the night the two Emperors are at the Castle.

The day 30 November the French fortify the hill, said, of the Santon, and occupy it with the 17° light, the same regiment that had defended Monte Negino in 1796, when it was a half-brigade, in order to dissuade Bagration to attack frontally to north; Bernadotte is arriving to Brünn from Iglau, after a march of 70 km.

Davout, meanwhile, left Vienna at 9 p.m. and has already covered the 70 km separating the capital from Nikolsburg. He must leave again in the night to make the last 40 km and arrive the evening of December 1 south of Brno (he will miss the Gudin brigade, which remained in Pressburg-Bratislava, to an additional day's march that, according to Davout *"would have to pull out the boots of the seven leagues"* to arrive in time). The Austro-Russian columns advanced slowly and, on the day of December 1, occupied the heights of Pratzen. Throughout the day they parade on the plateau, causing the Empereur, addressing Ségur, to exclaim: *"What a shameful movement! They are falling into a trap! They give themselves to me! Before tomorrow night this army will be mine!"*

Bonaparte did not cease, still, to resort to other pitfalls, ordering Bernadotte and Davout to halt out of sight of the enemy, the former west of Brno and the latter at Raygern. On the evening of December 1, the French line presented an oblique course, with the left forward, and appeared to be in defensive trim.

The night before the battle, Napoleon multiplies his lookouts sent on reconnaissance, to be sure that the adversaries are entering the trap, created by him. The battle of Austerlitz begins to look very similar to that of Castiglione (1796); one wing has been weakened to tempt the enemy to attack (then it was the left wing, this time it is the right) and two Corps are about to intervene by surprise (Davout's III Corps and Bernadotte's I Corps; at Castiglione it was Despinoy and Serurier).

THE PLANS OF AUSTERLITZ

How were the original orders of the Empereur? With good peace of mind of Franz von Weyrother it is quite appropriate to think that it was the French orders that could be decisive for the outcome of the battle. On November 21, the Empereur left Brno for a personal reconnaissance to the heights of Pratzen; it would not be the only one. He is not yet convinced of how, and where to give battle, since he does not know if he will be able to concentrate his forces in time. He orders Davout, accordingly, to take himself to Vienna with Friant and to send Gudin to Pressburg.

On the 27th, until the evening of November 28, after the Wischau affair, Napoleon takes himself to Posoritz to observe directly the adversary's order of battle. He takes with him, at the Old Post Office in Posoritz, his Marshals. It is said that before the con-sultation, Napoleon's subordinates probably have an argument. Marshals Murat and Soult, persuade Marshal Lannes, the most familiar with the Emperor, to advise Napoleon to retreat to more defensive positions. Lannes initially refuses, but at the insistence of the other two marshals writes a personal letter to the emperor. Before the letter is finished, Napoleon himself arrives at the post station, reads the letter and adds, *"Does Marshal Lannes want to retreat?"* Soult replies, *"In this way, Sire, the fourth army corps will double its forces."* Lannes, thinking that Soult was making him out to be a coward and that he only wanted to please Napoleon, burst into a rage, treating Soult as a *"bastard"* and continuing with the following words, *"these two persuaded me to write you the letter."* Napoleon glosses over the violent dispute, in which Lannes has offended Soult (he wanted to summon him to a duel) and, in the end, gives reason to the three, ordering a prudent retreat to Brno.

On November 29, Napoleon, has a conversation with the delegation of the Tsar, a fact that allows him further notes. His army forms a triangle with the northern vertex advanced towards the east and the base all in a westerly direction, a classic oblique order that allows the vertex to block an eventual attack in the direction of Brünn, while the right wing is theoretically arranged to strike on the flank an advancing army. As mentioned, the Coalition eventually shifted its right wing troops to the left of the road and, thus, prepared to enter the device devised by Bonaparte. On November 30, the Empereur inspects the works on the Santon and takes himself again to the plateau of Pratzen to observe the enemy approach; from the village of Pratzen he goes as far as Augezd and mentally notes the geography of the southern part of the battlefield.

In the meantime the adversaries put the famous Weyrother plan into action.

As for the plan, General Kutuzov was not too enthusiastic about the idea of Weyrother, (Austrian Chief of Staff Franz von Weyrother creator of the Allied Army battle plan). The Russian command had requested him as a liaison officer because he knew the Austerlitz territory well. Weyrother presented the two emperors with the arrangements, which were thought up on November 28 during their stay in Vyškov. However, it was still necessary to transmit the plan to the Allied subordinate commanders. From eight o'clock in the evening the room began to fill with officers. Weyrother unrolled a detailed map of the battlefield on the table. Then he began to explain, with triumphalist expressions, his plan; in which, by the way, he awaited the arrival of reinforcements under the command of Archduke Charles, the younger brother of the Austrian emperor. After the reading they say he scrutinized officers and generals, as the teacher investigates the faces of his students, when he finished his explanation. One of the generals present will note that it really had reminded him of his school years. *"He read aloud with such satisfaction that indicated the deepest conviction of his abilities and of our incompetence. He acted like a teacher giving lessons to his students. Kutuzov, sitting down had already fallen asleep and was snoring sonorously when we left."* Weyrother, therefore, was unable to capture the attention of his "students." When Kutuzov awakens, he will comment that the only viable option was not to give battle to the enemy. He believes, not having accurate information about the army of Archduke Charles, that the position on the Pratzen plateau is very advantageous for those defending. However, the Weyrother plan is finally accepted but, another major problem, its translation, from German to Russian, will take too long to reach the units; most of the generals obtained the instructions only at six in the morning.

Napoleon, in the meantime, is still uncertain about the time of the beginning of the enemy attack, but after having observed the adversary columns moving to Pratzen, on December 1st, he appears more serene. He had, in fact, guessed the Austro-Russian maneuver, that is, the descent from Pratzen, the attack on his right wing and ordered two flank attacks: the minor one to the south, made by Davout against the left flank of the Coalition, and the major one to the north, made with the bulk of the army against the Austrian right flank. He foresaw a huge stranglehold that would crush the advancing enemy. Already on the day of December 1, the Coalition forces move the large corps of General Buxhöwden, consisting of four columns: three Russian, Dokhturov, Langeron, Przbishevski and one Austrian under the command of Kienmayer. While slowly advancing from Pratzen, towards the Goldbach, they stop between the old vineyards (Staré Vinohrady) and the slope west of Hostieradek. For part of the day, the large corps of General Liechtenstein marched with them and at a certain point found himself bivouacked between two Russian columns, totally out of squad and beyond the point assigned to him by the Austro-Russian deployment, it is said due to a bad translation of the orders from German (but Liechtenstein did not know German?); his position will be corrected during the night.

In the north, Prince Bagration leans on the village of Posoritz, controlled, at a distance, by the cavalry of the French General Margaron, now aggregated to Soult's corps. The Russian Imperial Guard stops in the village of Krenowitz, that of the meeting. The eve of the Allied battle does not present good omens. Prince Czartoriski recounts one. *"Someone pointed out that the following day (November 20 or December 2 for us) was Monday, a day considered jellied in Russia. So, at the moment when the Emperor (the Czar) was passing, on horseback, over a grassy hump, his horse slipped and fell, knocking him from the saddle to the ground. It was nothing serious but was considered by some to be a very bad omen."*

At 8:30 p.m., Napoleon drew up the *"Dispositions générales pour la journee du 11 frimaire"*: *"Mr. Marshal Soult will give instructions for his three divisions to deploy beyond the ravine, at seven o'clock in the morning, so as to be ready to begin the day's maneuver, which will be a forward march in stages (battalions flanked in parallel or slightly out of phase. with the right wing advanced [...], His Highness Prince Murat will give the order [...] that the divisions be lined up, at seven o'clock in the*

morning, between the left of Marshal Soult and the right of Marshal Lannes, so as to occupy the least possible space, and so that, at the moment in which Marshal Soult will march, all that cavalry [...] will pass the stream that is in the center of the army. General Caffarelli is ordered to move at seven o'clock in the morning, with his division, to the right of the Suchet division, after passing the creek. The Suchet division will form on two lines, the Caffarelli division will form the same on two lines, each brigade forming one line, therefore the position currently occupied by the Suchet division will be sufficient for both divisions. Marshal Lannes will take care that the two divisions are always behind the hill so as not to be observed by the enemy. Mr. Marshal Bernadotte, with his two infantry divisions, will move at seven o'clock in the morning to the same position occupied today by the Caffarelli division, except that his left will stand behind the Santon, and will remain in column by regiment. M. Marshal Lannes will order the Grenadier division to bring itself in front of the present position, with its left behind the right of General Caffarelli. General Oudinot will make reconnaissance on the places where he will have to pass the stream, the same one that Marshal Soult will have passed. Marshal Davout, with the Friant division and the Dragoon division of General Bourcier, will leave at five in the morning from the Abbey of Raygern, to engage on the right of Marshal Soult . [...] At half past seven in the morning, the Marshals will report to the Emperor, at his bivouac to get new orders, according to the movements made by the enemy during the night [...] Until further notice, all troops will remain in the provisions indicated. Since Prince Murat's cavalry will have to occupy as little space as possible, they will form a column. [...] Each of the gentlemen marshals will transmit the orders concerning him that conform to these dispositions."

Note how the *"Dispositions générales"* are sparse and essential. Napoleon indicates to his Marshals the position to be occupied at seven o'clock in the morning and the space to be used, deferring to the seven-thirty briefing any further development. The Empereur's orders contrast with the minute details proposed by Franz von Weyrother's enemy plan. The chief of staff, who conceived the offensive, even proposed tactical objectives for each Austro-Russian column. The different approach hints at the different philosophies of the two General Staffs. Weyrother imagines an immobile enemy without any knowledge of battle tactics, Napoleon avoids burdening orders with tactical details, leaving the possibilities open to different situations.

This does not mean that Napoleon did not give tactical advice to his subordinates. So on November 26 he instructed Soult on how to deal with the Russians but, knowing that everything does not always succeed a priori he adds to the order an *"autant que faire se pourra"* (assuming it can be done); in the end then really, Soult will not be able to follow that advice. The order of the 26th, however, is a clear example of what would later be renamed the *"ordre mixte"*. According to this instruction, each brigade was to deploy with its first regiment in battle (i.e. in line), the second regiment in serried columns by divisions. The artillery was to be between the two battalions of the regiment in battle, with a few pieces placed on the wings of the same regiment, right and left. Cavalry squadrons were to be deployed behind each brigade in order *"to be able to pass through the intervals, pursue the enemy, and face the Cossacks."* This is a clear example of what Napoleon meant by coordination between various arms, having both firepower and mobility at his disposal; addressed to Soult he had added: *"With this order of battle you will find yourself able to face the enemy both with line fire and with columns to oppose his."* On December 1, 1805, in his instructions to General Vandamme, Soult very freely adapted the imperial advice by specifying the role of the light infantry: *"...which will be held a hundred paces in front of the two brigades, which will be formed in battle for the first line and in battalion column for the second line."* The morning of the battle then, Soult, will give different provisions to Saint-Hilaire: *"only the light infantry will form in battle, while the two line brigades will deploy one right and the other left of the light infantry in column by platoon distance divisions."* In the end, according to a study by Colin, each division, which was to attack Pratzen, was deployed

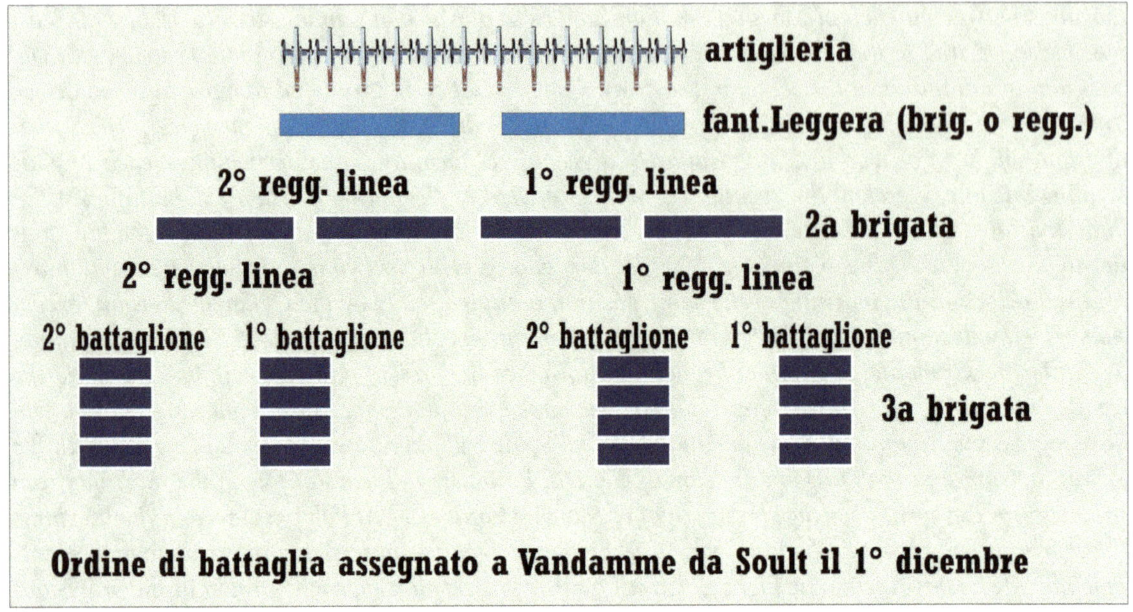

in three lines of battalions deployed in column, so as to obtain very compact formations, occupying little space and very mobile, but ready then to deploy in line where necessary (and in fact the attack would be so rapid and lethal that there would be no need to change formation). During the night between 1 and 2 December, Savary reports on the reconnaissance carried out, informing Napoleon of the arrival of new troops in Tellnitz. Napoleon wants to see for himself and leaves his command on the top of the hill of Zuran, he goes to Girzikowitz, also risking to fall into the hands of Cossacks. He understands that the bulk of the enemy forces are now south of an imaginary line that joins the villages of Pratzen to Krenowitz, with the intention of breaking through the French line at Tellnitz. To the north he believes only Bagration remained. In fact, the Empereur does not have a certain idea, but an intuition, strengthened also by the noises of the adversaries' moving caissons, which echo in the icy night. By dint of depleting his right wing now l'Empereur fears to be a victim of his own *"trap"*. he changes his original plan, considering the Austro-Russian forces scarce in the north: the I corps of Bernadotte instead of gathering behind the Santon must aim at Girzikowitz and follow Soult, the Saint-Hilaire division of the IV corps must flow to Puntowitz instead of Girzikowitz, where Vandamme will pass. Soult now directs his pressure much further south no longer with his advanced right wing, but with his left straight against the Pratzen.

Above all, he modifies the order of battle for Davout's III Corps, knowing that Gudin may arrive late on December 2 and that Bourcier and Friant may not be able to effectively counterattack the enemy flank. Supported by the Legrand division of IV Corps, Davout now received orders to defend the Goldbach line at Tellnitz and Sokolnitz to slow down enemy pressure and to facilitate the attack of his main mass of maneuver. Adjustments made, Napoleon again sends Savary on reconnaissance towards Tellnitz, before taking a well-deserved rest.

The battle is now going to hit the Pratzen, the "soft underbelly" of the enemy, to cut the Austro-Russian deployment in two and to repel the strong enemy left wing against the frozen ponds of Satschan and Mönitz. Despite the *"trap"* and Napoleon's brilliant insights, a margin of chance remains. The Empereur is worried about Davout's weakness in the field, and the recognition of the enemy force by the number of fires lit does not seem very accurate; fewer fires may have been lit to deceive the French, or the night fog may be hiding distant lights.

The French, on the eve of the battle, celebrate the emperor in reconnaissance to the units; the cries of *"Evviva"* mix with the fires of the flashlights... someone even thinks of setting fire to the roofs of the Girzikowitz huts to better celebrate Napoleon. Then the army tries to rest. However, not all of them will be able to sleep, as Paul Dieudonné Thiébault, brigadier co-commander of the 2nd brigade of the Saint-Hilaire division, recollects: *"Returning to Kolbenitz (sic), around eleven o'clock in the evening, I found the order to have my brigade take up arms at three o'clock in the morning, to bring it in front of that village, reuniting it with the rest of the division. This order was ridiculous, for it would not be daylight until eight o'clock, and, by allowing the troops another three hours' rest, nothing was compromised; but under the uniform one obeys, one does not argue, even if one thinks otherwise. As for Richebourg and myself, we found it not worth while to sleep three hours; we spent the rest of that night, playing Chess, the last night which, for poor Richebourg, would precede that of eternity."*

▲ Portrait of Louis Nicolas Davout (1770-1823). Work by Tito Marzocchi de Belluci

AUSTERLITZ: THE BATTLE

THE REACTIVE OR ELASTIC DEFENSE IN TELLNITZ

During the first phase of the battle, Napoleon set himself a goal: to resist requests for reinforcements from the generals in charge of the defense of secondary sectors, such as the right wing. **It is the principle of the economy of forces applied to the battle**, rather than to the campaign, that is, to have an adequate reserve of troops ready to take advantage to deal a death blow to the enemy.

On the night of December 1, the French right wing included only the 6,000 troops of the Legrand division, detached from Soult's corps, which occupied the long stretch of front between Tellnitz and Kobelnitz. The rest of the center-north front counts 60000 French. Davout in that moment arrives to Raygern with units in suffering for the forced march; Friant, on December 2, enters in battle with only 4000 men of the 7000, that were available at the end of November. The weakness of Davout imposes to Napoleon the necessity to resort to a perfect timing between the phase of preparation and the unleashing of the decisive attack; if this last one happened too late, the French right wing would be irreparably perforated by the Austro-Russian raiders, if instead it was too premature it would leave the time to disengage to the adversaries on the southern front.

On December 1, at 8:30 in the evening, Davout receives the operative order from Berthier who orders to leave from Raygern Abbey (Rajhrad) at 5:00 a.m. to connect to Soult's right wing with the Friant and Bourcier divisions. Davout has already understood that he will have to rely only on his meager forces. He will have to resort to using all the resources of the terrain to slow down the

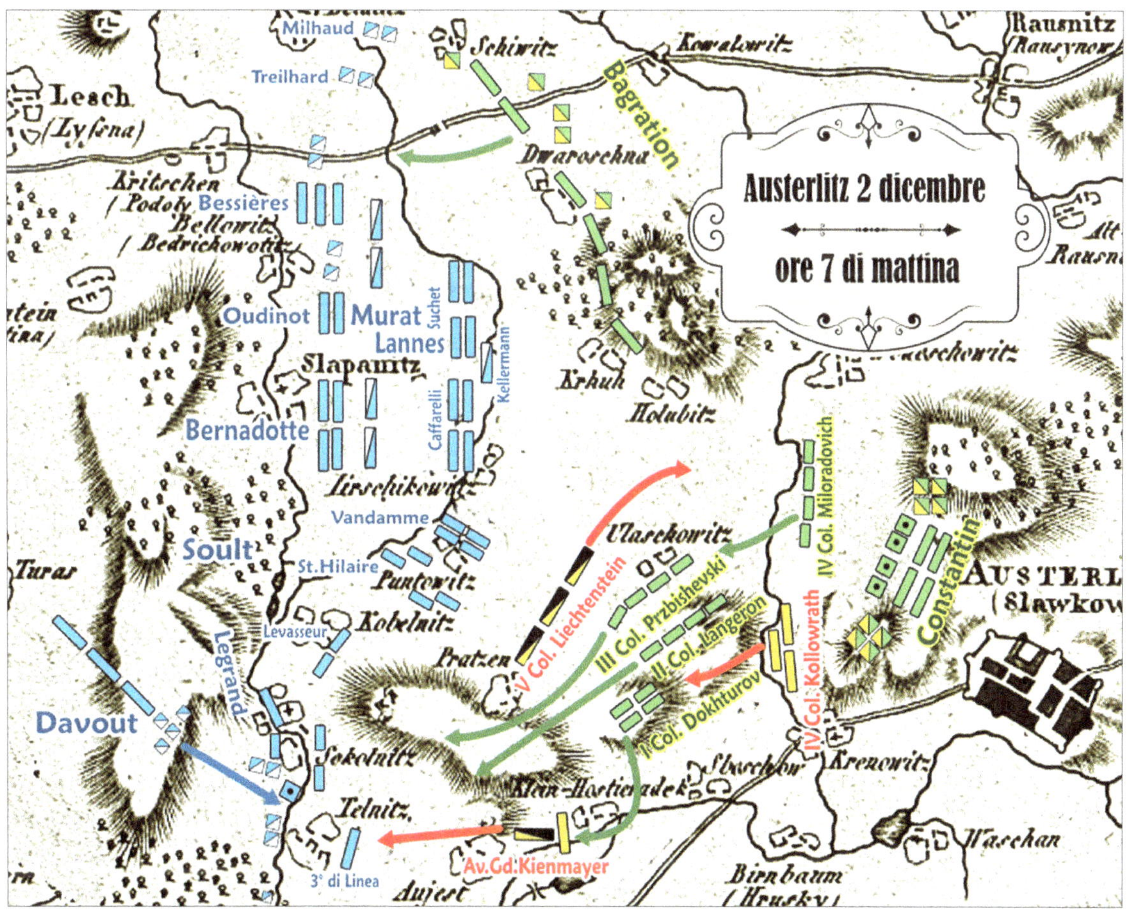

Austro-Russian advance. His battle will take place between the villages of Tellnitz and Sokolnitz; Tellnitz is the anchorage point of the French right and it will be there, shortly before 8 am, that the first contact with the enemy will occur. The settlement, located east of the Goldbach stream on the left bank, is surrounded by crops and vineyards; to the south it borders the vast frozen ponds of Satschan and Mönitz. Eight hundred meters to the north, however, on the right bank of the Goldbach is the village of Sokolnitz, which stretches into an estate, with a palace, with a park, bounded by walls, 600 meters long and 300 wide called "pheasantry", because of the game farms. While waiting for Davout, Soult's troops (3rd Legrand Division) are in charge of the defense; the division general has sent Colonel Schobert with 1600 men of the 3rd line regiment to occupy Tellnitz at night, providing to drive out the Austrian cavalry that was placed between the houses. Between Tellnitz and Sokolnitz about 300 Tirailleurs from Corsica (Levasseur brigade) and the Po are deployed; finally 500 sabers of the Chasseurs 19th and 26th horse regiments (General Margaron) support the infantry.

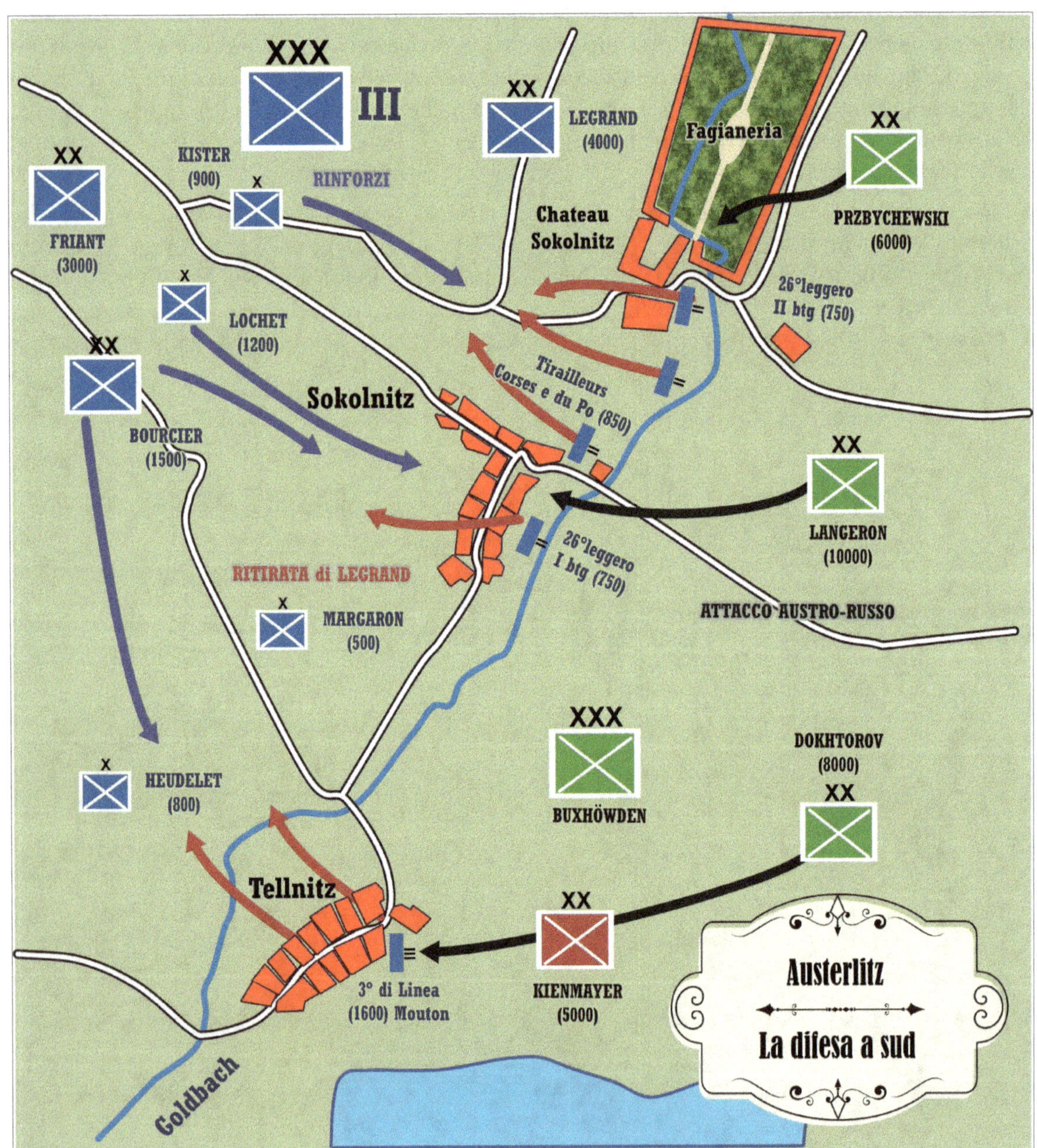

The first shots are heard in the night of December 1, during a shootout between Austrians and French soldiers. At 19 o'clock in the evening, a squadron of O'Reilly cavalry (Kienmayer's vanguard) appears in reconnaissance in front of Tellnitz. There is no moon and a thick fog increases the darkness of the night. The Corsican Tirailleurs outposts are overrun and a few bolder cavalrymen penetrate the alleys of Tellnitz, fighting with the Corsicans and the 1st battalion of the 3rd Line. The resistance of the Tirailleurs and their commander Ornano, allows General Legrand to send the 2nd and 3rd Line battalions to reinforce the Goldbach line. Commander Hulot and his Tirailleurs du Pô are also engaged in repelling the Allied vanguards at Sokolnitz.

The cavalry of the Austro-Russian vanguard, the Hussars of Hessen-Homburg, has warned Kienmayer of the new French positions and the general orders his units to occupy Tellnitz, so as to open the way for Dokhturov's Russian column, which is coming. After a pause of several hours, the firing resumes, around two or three in the morning. Field Marshal Kienmayer's Austrian corps attempts to push back Marshal Legrand's troops and take the village of Tellnitz held by the French 3rd Line Regiment. The fighting between the Austrians (now there are the border Szekler, the infantry) and the French (3rd Line) becomes immediately bitter. The French drive back their enemies and manage to repel attempts by Kienmayer's Grenzer to recapture the village. Finally, a part of this corps manages to break the French ranks, but without cannon support, the Austrians are forced to retreat with great losses.

Thanks to that night shooting, Napoleon realizes that the Allied line extends much further south than he had thought. He sends Savary ahead, to gather news. Based on that information, Napoleon makes the final changes to his plan. He sends a letter to Marshal Davout with orders to head not toward Tuřany (Turas) but toward Sokolnitz. In the final version of his orders, the emperor relies on the Kobelnitz-Tellnitz line of defense. He knows that the French would be clearly outnumbered, against the Allies, in the extreme south of the battlefield. He hopes to occupy his enemies as long as possible to execute his action in the center, then take the Pratzen plateau and outflank the Allied rear guard.

Soult assigns the 3rd of Line to the defense of Tellnitz, where Colonel Schobert will build a defensive support point with the support of the Tirailleurs of Corsica of Ornano. The Levasseur brigade (18th and 75th Line) are sent in front of Kobelnitz, as a sector reserve. The rest of the Merle brigade (26th Light Regiment) is sent south of Kobelnitz, while the Po Tirailleurs will remain at Sokolnitz. Margaron's mounted Chasseurs and their mounted artillery will descend toward Tellnitz. At dawn on December 2, the French right wing is only defended by 2400 soldiers and 6 cannons; it will be reinforced by another 3800 men and 9 cannons when Friant reaches Goldbach.

The attack of the allied columns is triggered at 7 am. In front of Tellnitz fights Kienmayer, with his five battalions and fifteen squadrons, which are paraded, along the pond of Mönitz, to attack the cavalry of Margaron, south of the village. The Austrians attacked, forced to ford the torrent, passing several ditches and climbing a slope covered with vineyards and houses, on top of which the 3rd Line and the Corsicans lurked, behind occasional shelters. The arrival of Russian reinforcements causes the loss of Tellnitz. Legrand sends the 26th light reinforcement, but this does not arrive at Tellnitz; instead it is diverted to the defense of Sokolnitz. The 3rd Line, now reduced to 1200 men, is pushed west of the Goldbach by the Austrians and about 3000 Russians of Dokhturov who followed them, after arriving at Tellnitz at seven in the morning.

The French are forced, now, to retreat and regroup, then, near the Goldbach. The retreat, according to the canons of reactive defense, is protected by the Chasseurs of Margaron and the 1st Dragoon Regiment, sent by Davout, who perfectly understood the crisis in the south and ordered Friant to head on Tellnitz. About nine o'clock, the 15th Light and the 108th Line (Heudelet Brigade, about 800 men) succeed in reoccupying the village at the bayonet; the success is short-lived. While Lieutenant General Dokhturov prepares his infantry for the new assault, the French quickly gear up for defense and fortify themselves in the village houses. Between Sokolnitz and Tellnitz, a hullabaloo breaks out between friendly troops, confused and disoriented by the fog and smoke from rifle and cannon fire; the French shoot at each other. Dokhturov takes advantage of that chaos and reconquers the disputed village. The fact, not uncommon, is thus recounted in the history of the 15th Light Infantry.

"Taking advantage of that success, the vaulters of the 15th Light came out of the village, climbed a high ground in front and vigorously repulsed a charge by the Hesse-Homburg hussars. The 108th came out into the open, in turn, and moved to their left, when it was caught behind by a well-fed fire that forced it back into Tellnitz: it was the 26th light (Legrand division) that, positioned along the creek and unable to distinguish colors because of the fog, had taken the 108th for Russians and had opened fire. This misunderstanding also forced the vaulters back into the village, from which a furious attack by the Russians drove the French back again. The Austrian cavalry immediately crossed Tellnitz and threw themselves against the knights of Bourcier and Margaron, whose horses were tired from the marches. Heudelet, having reconstituted his troops, came, with his fire to the aid of the cavalry, and contained the enemy. It was 10 o'clock in the morning;"

On Davout's orders, the French formed a defensive line south of Sokolnitz, which was attacked by Langeron's 10,000 Russians. Defending the village of Tellnitz is only Colonel Pouget with his two battalions of the 26th Light; they are soon overrun and forced to retreat. *"During the battle of Tellnitz I had much to suffer from the indocility of the horse I was riding which, frightened by the hiss of the balls whirling around its ears and between its legs, would not allow me to go where I thought my presence was necessary. Chef-de-bataillon Brillat offered me his, which I quickly accepted. The moment I set foot on the ground, I felt myself covered with earth and stones, which were thrown in my face with such force that I bled and was almost blinded. A cannonball had fallen three paces from me. I mounted the most docile horse and rode to the center of my regiment, which I encouraged by voice and example, to honorably defend its position, although in a cold mind the task seemed to be beyond its strength."* Colonel François-René Cailloux Baron Pouget

When Przbichevski occupies the Sokolnitz Palace Pheasantry at 9:30 a.m., all the strongholds of the French right wing are in Russian hands. A relative peace is established after ten in the morning. Later, the French will retreat towards Otmarov. Tellnitz and Sokolnitz remain in the hands of the Russians. But Napoleon's soldiers have fulfilled the required task - to occupy and stop for a few hours a larger army.

> The pastor of Tellnitz finds himself in the middle of the clash: *"Bullets were flying inside the rectory, through the windows, and there was incredible damage everywhere. There were dozens of corpses in the village. After the armistice, many Frenchmen stopped in the village to ensure the burial of the fallen soldiers."* Since then, about 140 bodies rest in the village's mass grave. The inhabitants of Tellnitz, then, had to deliver, against their will, to the French all the bread, meat but also other food. *"They took two horses, four cows, a heifer, sixteen pigs, forty-four flasks of wine, two hundred rations of oats and many other things from the parish yard."*

The danger is considerable and the defense here is at risk of no longer being so "elastic". Napoleon could fall victim of his own trap. Luckily for him, the Austro-Russians are exhausted and intoxicated with victory; they do not pursue. Buxhöwden, in command of the southern sector, waits for the columns of Przbichevski and Langeron to connect to the south with Dokhturov and Kienmayer, but this wait will prove fatal. At that moment the bulk of the French division Friant arrives, launched against Sokolnitz, with the two brigades Kister and Lochet. Lochet is probably the best general of this division, Davout himself considers him *"exceptional officer in everything"*, his colleagues admire him for the discipline he knows how to give to his units. Lochet throws into Sokolnitz the 48th Line, a

▲ The castle of Sokolnitz today. Courtesy by John Callahan

mass of 1400 men, many veterans, 783 have between 10 and 15 years of service, under the command of Colonel Joseph Barbanegre, a fervent Republican. The 48th is supported by the Piedmontese and Italians of the 111th line, together they drive the enemy out of the alleys of Sokolnitz, despite an obvious numerical inferiority.

In the meantime Kister attacks the palace and the pheasantry, with Davout observing in admiration the fury of the French attack, especially of the 33rd line, followed by the 15th light. In the palace park, Russian resistance is considerable, and while further south, Sokolnitz changes masters more than once, the attack between Kobelnitz and Sokolnitz sets the pace.

One anecdote concerns the eagle of the 33rd. It is saved by Private Putigny, under the nose of Buxhöwden's Russians. When the 33rd was forced to retreat, under threat of outflanking, by jumping across a ditch, wide and deep, the imperial eagle detached itself from the pole and fell into the muddy and nauseating water. Left behind, Putigny descends into the ditch and, with water up to his belt, searches for the symbol of the Empire while the Russians shoot at him. Finally, groping, he finds his Eagle, escapes under fire. He runs like a madman and reaches his comrades who thought they had lost him and "the bird" (sic). In the evening at the bivouac, while he is drying his uniform stained with blackish mud, an aide-de-camp comes to tell him that the Emperor wants him to report. The Sovereign is there, dressed in his gray redingote, talking to General Friant who has told him the heroic anecdote. Putigny approaches, Napoleon grabs his ear and says, *"So, I hear you're going fishing with your flag? Don't worry, it's even more beautiful than before. You're a good boy and I'm awarding you the star of my Legion of Honor!"*.

After a grueling morning of assaults Davout unleashes the decisive attack at 12:30. The Russians, exhausted, are pushed back to the north, to the palace and to the pheasantry. They will be cut off by Napoleon's attack on Pratzen, while further south Kienmayer and Dokhturov will retreat in the direction of Hostieradek, towards the frozen ponds.

THE LION'S LEAP

As mentioned in his memoirs of the 1805 campaign, Langeron severely judges Weyrother's plan afferming that: *" ... with a skilful commander and experienced subordinates in front, who commanded troops that were not novices, it was absurd to hope to win with a simple wing attack after having extended the front for about eight Verste (about 8 km) [...] between the cavalry of the Center and the Fourth column there were about two Verste (2 km) unmanned by anyone. Could such an error have escaped Napoleon?"*

Indeed, it did not escape Napoleon's notice that the supposed weakness of the Central deployment, given due calculation. However, the decisive attack must be launched at the right point, when the entire Austro-Russian left wing will no longer have any chance to repel and strengthen the Pratzen, attacked by the French. It does not escape Savary, then, the description of the scene which shows itself to his eyes early in the morning of December 2. All the marshals surrounded Bonaparte quivering with haste to begin operations, while he resisted pressure and invited them to wait a moment longer. Ségur notes, *"Already [...] their attack had begun at Tellnitz and Sokolnitz [...] and it was not yet eight o'clock; silence and darkness still reigned over the rest of the lines, when, suddenly, the sun appeared on the Pratzen plateau, dispelling the fog..."* Dawn breaks over the eastern horizon and a red sun breaks through the fog on the hills above Holubitz. The incredible scene dumbfounds everyone, including Napoleon. The exceptional nature of this moment will cause the Austerlitz sun to become a legend.

The artillery officer Levavasseur, 2nd regiment on horseback, attached to Murat's cavalry recounts: *"The Emperor gives the order to bring the artillery forward. At this point, our one hundred and fifty guns set off, passing between the intervals of the battalions of the first three lines. They will place themselves in battery, fifty or one hundred paces in front of the infantry. I have executed this movement, and, as I command my light artillery, I place myself a little ahead of the line of guns. I find, then, that the whole of the enemy's artillery is executing the same movement as we are; a battery of ten pieces comes to take up a position on my left, catching me a little on the flank. General Kellermann, commander of the light cavalry, deploys in the midst of the several batteries, to defend them. All these movements are made with the order and precision, which one usually sees only in a magazine at the Champ de Mars. We were well deployed, and yet the firing did not begin. Finally, a cannon shot starts from our right: at the same time, a frightful bombardment begins, on either side; I direct the fire of my battery on the one I have mentioned and whose balls, fired too high, pass over my head. Yet they have already killed one of my brigadiers, and a Marechal de Logis has been thrown to the ground; a ball bounces off my pieces and smashes a caisson. The smoke of the enemy cannon, pouring over us like a dense fog, prevents me from seeing the effect of my shots. In order to recognize it, I throw myself so far forward that my gunners cannot understand how I am not hit, being in the line of sight of the enemy: they do not reason by reflecting that they are below the curve described by the balls. From there I rectified the firing of my men several times and used the machine gun to electrocute those I had in range."*

The most anxious to begin seems to be Soult with his corps of 16,000 men. He claims that in ten minutes he will conquer the Pra-tzen and Bonaparte says to wait a little longer, a quarter of an hour more and then gives the order. Thus begins what some historians have called the "leap or the lion's paw", the unexpected event that upsets the Austro-Russian plans.

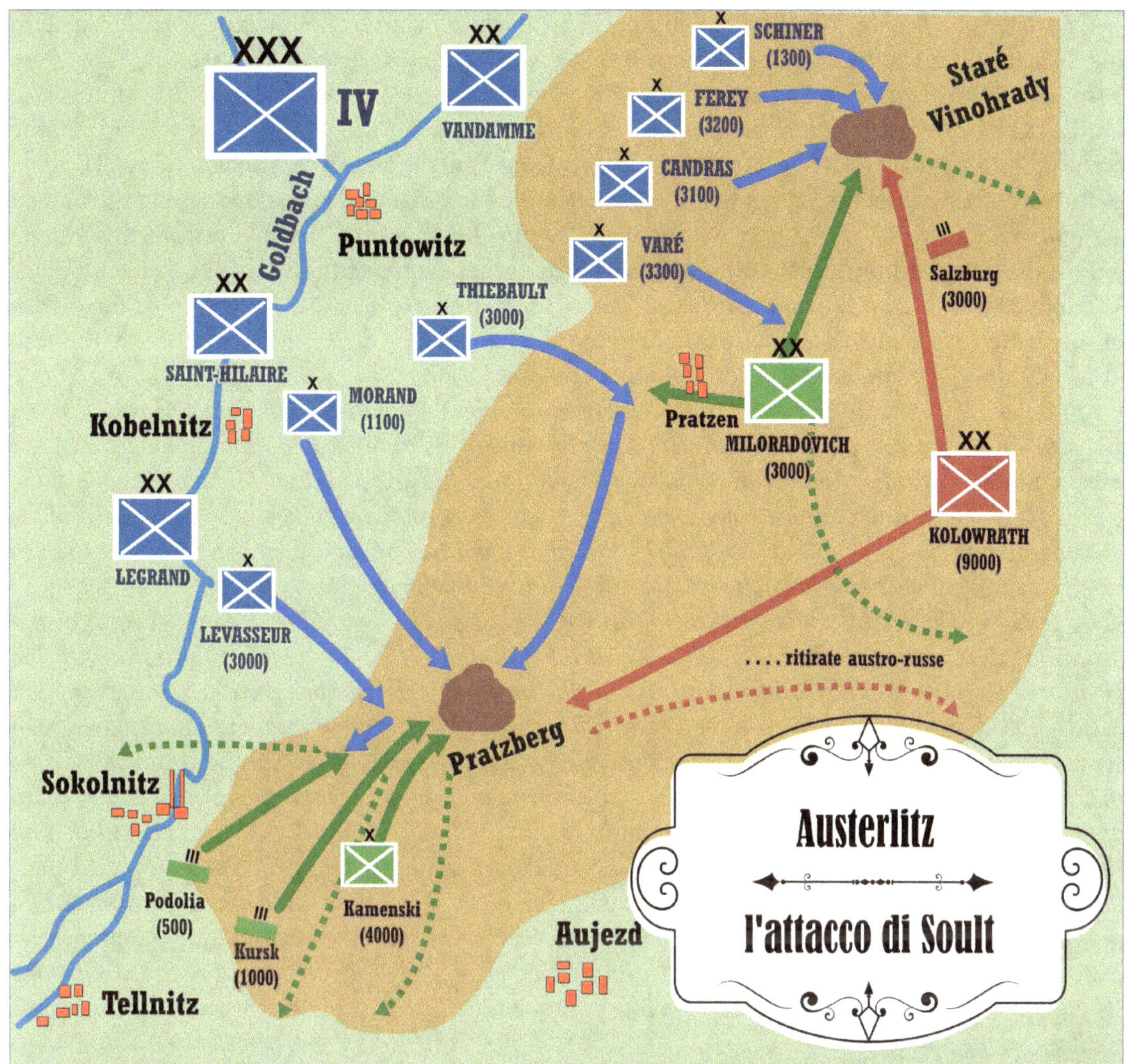

The beginning of the Austro-Russian hostilities are told to us by the history of the 9th Infantry Regiment, at the time Czartorinski: *"The fourth column split in two to give the first three columns time to reach their positions. At 7:30 in the morning, while the third column was aiming at Sokolnitz Castle on the left and the fifth column was aiming at Blasowitz on the right, our objective was to go over Pratzen in the direction of Puntowitz. At its head marched the Russian infantry, followed by two Austrian brigades, Jurczek and Rottermund. Two Russian battalions and two squadrons of Archduke Johann's Dragoons formed the vanguard. The head of the column had just reached the right summit of Pratzen, which had just been abandoned by the rear-guard of the 3rd Column, when we noticed, beyond Pratzen, two enemy columns approaching. Our advance guard quickened its pace by crossing the village, occupying the bridge after it before the enemy tirilleurs; it crossed it and took up position in the vicinity of a church, on a small hill beyond the village. Kutusov's order was to secure, at all costs, the heights to the left of Pratzen. For that reason he had diverted the columns slightly to the left when a third enemy column, Drouet Division of Bernadotte's Corps, was sighted and appeared to be advancing toward the heights to the right of the village. As the Russians deployed into position to meet this other threat, the enemy had already climbed the hills to the left of Pratzen and taken the village. Kutuzov then ordered the Austrian Jurczek and Rottermund brigades to retake the heights, where the French had just pushed back the Russian vanguard. Here the battle was decided."*

In reality, the Austro-Russian IV column, under the command of Kollowrath, was subjected to the assault of the Saint-Hilaire division; subjected is not the correct term because the Allies were advancing towards the French lines, to pass the Goldbach. It is therefore a real and genuine clash on the field. The Austrians march safe, they have not even done reconnaissance of the terrain, the scene of training maneuvers in 1804. According to Langeron, the lack of reconnaissance will be fatal to the central device, commanded by Miloradovich; they advance without knowing that the French are 300 meters away, it seems they do not even have loaded muskets. The soldiers of Saint-Hilaire fall on the vanguard of the IV column that improvises a defense of the village of Pratzen. Major Toll, sent ahead by the Russian command, had, in fact, time to warn Miloradovich of the arrival of the French; he deployed his vanguard between the houses of Pratzen and, to the south, the rest. Thiebault, in his memoirs, describes the first attack on the Pratzen plateau: *"Saint-Hilaire had told me that the village should only be occupied by enemy outposts. I had charged Colonel Mazas with his 1st battalion with the assault; however, with some additional precaution, I had Mazas followed by the other battalions, arranged in line by battalion masses. I did this well because [...] the battalions of the Novgorod regiment and the Apsheron regiment [...], sent to occupy the village as the vanguard of the 4th column, had had time to move in front of the village and lie down on their stomachs so as not to be seen as we approached. The moment Mazas began the battle march, they sprang to their feet, while our troops were halted by a wide ravine, in front of the village. Those fired at close range with such a deadly fire that, from surprise and fright, the entire 1st Battalion of the 14th Line began to straggle."* The History of the Line Regiment tells it this way, *"In the meantime, we climbed the Pratzen high ground at a charge. A Russian regiment was defending this village. We arrived in column and, deployed on a somewhat oblique line, our left was, when the deployment was over, ten paces from the enemy, whom the readiness of our fire soon put in rout; in spite of the reinforcement of other troops rushed to the aid of the Russians, the 14th was able to maintain the position it had conquered ... It must be said that, at first, we were deceived by a trick of the Russians. When our battalion fire ceased, a number of Russians threw themselves on the ground, and when we overtook them, they got up and took us from behind, as did their wounded, at least those who could still use their weapons. We were forced to adopt a rigorous attitude so as not to be exposed to that danger any longer. However, they often renewed the same stratagem. In an hour's time, however, we broke through the line to the enemy's reserve, between the Center and the left wing."*

In spite of the surprise, the infantry of Apsheron and Novgorod are pushed back inside the village, by the rest of the brigade, while Morand is climbing towards the top of the hill (Pratzberg); it is about 9.30 a.m. The battle is still open. Kutuzov, who is watching the French attack, throws an Austrian battalion from Kollowrath into the fray, behind which the Russian battalions can regroup. The Austrian battalion, although formed by recruits, manages to stop Saint-Hilaire's progression. At that juncture, the Russian general Kamenski, who was descending towards Tellnitz and heard the shooting behind him, without waiting for orders from his superior Langeron, turns around and goes back towards the village. It is about 10 o'clock when Morand's brigade lines up in a southwesterly direction to face the advancing Kamenski, while Thiebault's brigade is positioned perpendicular to Morand's to receive the attack of the Austrian battalion. The situation is critical for the French in the southern Pratzen sector. Without counting the Levasseur brigade, they have only 5000 men against the 10000 of the Kolowrath and Kamenski columns.

In front is Morand, followed by Thiébault with the following order of advance: 1st battalion of the 14th, the 36th regiment; the 2nd battalion of the 14th, which had pursued two Russian battalions, had yet to be reorganized and could not follow the brigade. Morand, alone with the 10th Light Regiment faced the entire Kamenski brigade; Morand was outflanked to the right and left, risking an attack from behind. At that critical moment, General Saint-Hilaire takes the 1st batt. of the 14th Line and

▲ Pratzen heights to the north, in the middle you can see the Santon chapel and a little further to the right the Bosenitz church (Tvarozna). Courtesy by John Callahan

has it flanked, at a running pace, on the right of the 1st batt. of the 10th Light, to balance the ongoing fight. Then the Thiébault brigade arrives and is flanked by Morand. General Paul Dieudonné Thiébault tells us: *"That Kamenski brigade, which was estimated at 4-5000 soldiers, had four regiments massed and was coming towards us on our left, on the Krenowitz side, behind the line formed by Morand. When I saw them advancing, I stopped my three remaining battalions the moment General Saint-Hilaire arrived. With our telescopes, we examined the masses as they moved forward, but we could not see anything to announce the enemy. But at a certain point we heard their music, and shortly afterwards, an officer of that regiment came within shouting distance: - Don't shoot, we are Bavarians. - The moment he was sure that we had understood, he returned to his regiment. - Ah - said General Saint-Hilaire to me - what shall we do? - My general,- I answered, with a liveliness that was not at all usual for me, -these Bavarians are suspicious, and this officer who did not dare to approach us seems to me to be even more so. - Would you risk -he resumed- shooting at allies of the Empereur? - And for what reason should allies of the Emperor march against us? - He insisted on trying to make me understand how such an error would be fatal; I replied that an attack by surprise would be disastrous and added that I would give instructions to the men, as if they were enemies, and then I would personally go on reconnaissance. In fact, we saw neither Bavarian uniforms nor their commanders, although it was rumored that a Bavarian corps had joined us during the night.*

In all haste I deployed the 36th Line, in support of Morand, which formed the pivot around which I maneuvered by placing it in column, while, to the left of my line, I placed the 2nd battalion of the 14th, to be able to oppose a reserve mass against those who were advancing against us and to have troops to oppose eventual cavalry, without altering my line. Morand placed three of his six divisional artillery pieces in position, I deployed the last three in the interval between my two battalions of the 36th Line, at which time I was under the command of Chef-de-bataillon Fontenay. The Emperor sent us six 12-pounder pieces judging our position to be in danger. I immediately deployed them on both flanks of the 36th regiment, masking them with infantry platoons. I then set off, belly down, to go and see who was coming. "

It seems clear that this is the decisive point of the battle, already won by the French to the north and on the Pratzen. In fact, if the Russian columns in the south, by now masters of Tellnitz and Sokolnitz, made a front in the north-east, threatening Napoleon's flank, they could seriously overturn what had happened until then. The arrival of Kamenski and Langeron is not an event to be overlooked. Oudinot's special corps will be sent downstream to plug the breach.

Meanwhile, Thiébault and Morand meet, both with the same intentions, in advanced reconnaissance. *"One of the officers of those regiments was joined by an officer, who came from the Kamenski brigade; they chatted a moment together and hurried, one to return to his troops, the other to join his own. If there had still been any doubt, this event had removed it, and, after telling Morand about it, I left him, saying, - Don't take care of these any more, I'll take care of them.... "*

It is at this point that one of those episodes occurs, frequent in Napoleonic battles, which see the artillery as the protagonist. The episode is cited by General Thiebault: *"I ordered Commander Fontenay ... to load all pieces with machine guns and buckshot and, responding to the objection that this would damage them, I replied: - it is enough that they last ten minutes! - I then had the aiming of the pieces checked to shoot at 10 or 20 toises (about 20-40 m). I ordered that 10 machine-gun cartridges and 10 buckshot cartridges be placed near each piece, in order to have a faster rate of fire; I reminded my troops to aim well before firing, to aim at the men's belts, at the center of the platoons, so as not to miss a single rifle shot; after having renewed these appeals to the last, I let those formidable masses approach at the established distance and, abruptly, I released the nine masked pieces from the troops who, together with the rifles, began a fire so destructive, which had never been seen [...] It was irrefutable that the enemy troops, believing they were attacking infantry without artillery, had been surprised by as many as nine large caliber pieces that were firing with extreme rapidity [...] I noted to my satisfaction how each cannonade opened gaps between the crammed troops attacking, and the four regiments attacking me dispersed in masses of fugitives [...]"*

Having arrived, finally, on the highest part of the Pratzen heights, Saint-Hilaire's French now dominate a vast horizon. Far away, on the left, come the echoes of the firing of Lannes' corps, and before that, halfway up, about two kilometers away, one can hear Bernadotte's first division fighting against the reserve of Grand Duke Constantin. Soult's troops succeeded, in the end, in pushing back the enemies on the Pratzen thanks to the concurrence of the Levasseur brigade, which attacked on the flank the Russian regiment of Kursk and part of Langeron's column, which came to the rescue of Kamenski. On the draft, Levasseur also drove back the Podolia regiment (Przbichewski column) inside the Sokolnitz pheasantry.

Further north of the village of Pratzen, Vandamme had an easier time. Before the assault of his Candras brigade, the 3000 Russians commanded by Miloradovich had already been repeatedly hit by French attacks. When Candras attacked, on the positions of Staré Vinohrady (the old vineyard), there were only 1000 Russians; according to logic and also according to Langeron the Russian line would be wiped out in less than half an hour. Vandamme's progression in the "old vineyard" now collides with the mighty Salzburg regiment, IR 23, of Colonel Baron von Sterndahl. *"The heights are full of mouths of fire,"* recount the infantrymen of the 4th Line Regiment, *and the enemy has formed on several lines. His position, his skill, would have frightened less determined troops; but nothing could stop these braves. Thrown headlong, they break through the first line and take its artillery. The second line, supported by mounted troops, experiences the same fate. In vain the third line, which a mammoth favors, masking its movements, maneuvers to get around us on the left; it is attacked in front by the 4th Line and on the flank by the 24th Light, under the orders of Brigadier Schiner."*

According to Soult's report, the 4th and 28th lines, along with the 24th light (Ferey and Schiner brigades) bayonet attacked the Austrian infantry and pushed them back, forcing them to repair behind Miloradovich's Russian infantry to regroup. Miloradovich himself attempts an attack but, in turn,

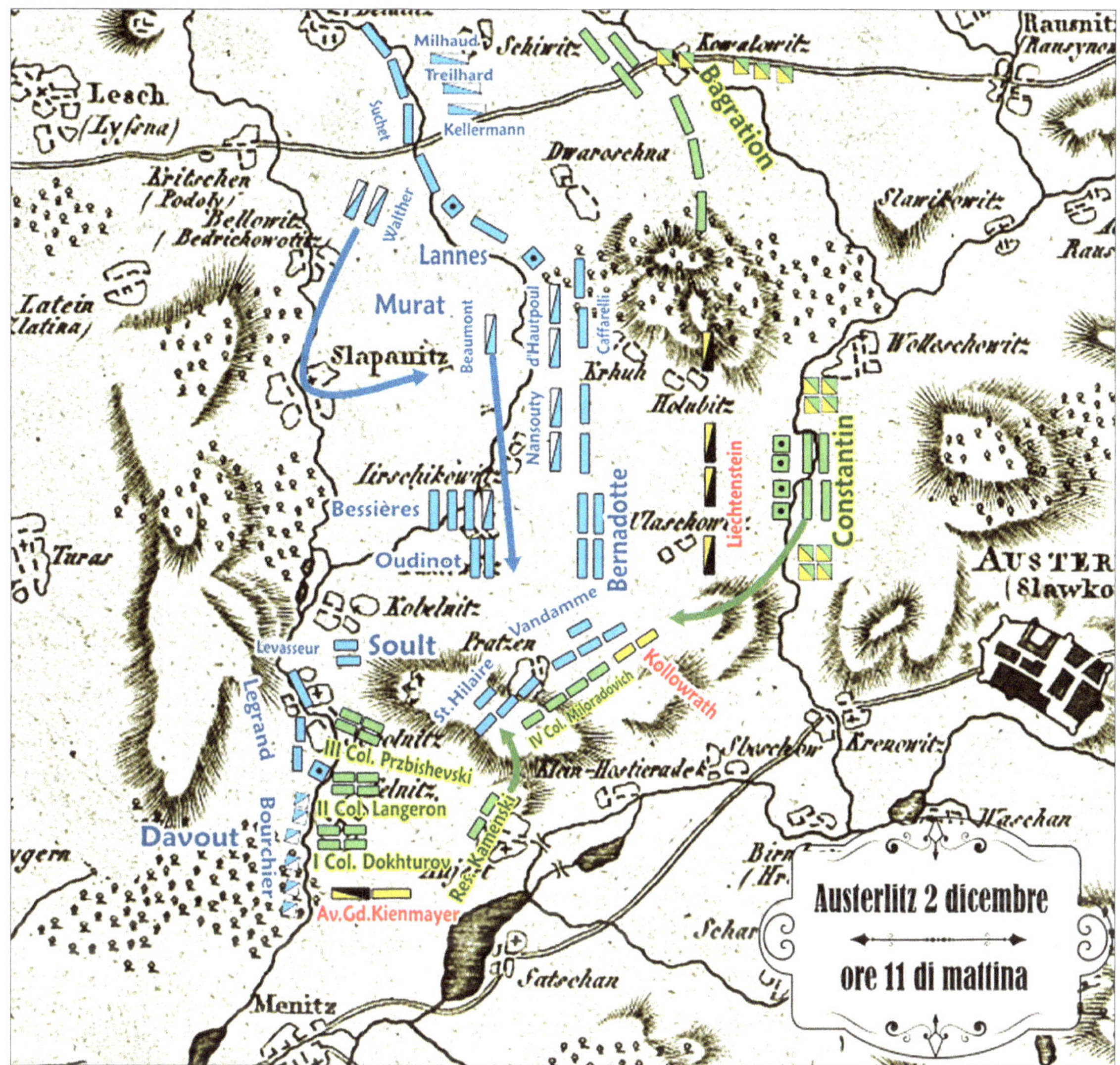

must repair behind the Austrians to reorder the ranks; however, the Salzburg is in full disorder and this marks the fate of Miloradovich, who must abandon the battlefield.

The battle is described by Major Mahlern, commander of the 1st battalion of the Kerpen line regiment (Kolowrath column): *"On December 2, at 7 am, there was such a thick fog that you could not see 50 steps. We heard loud gunfire, but we could not tell whether it was ours or the enemy attacking [...] because of the fog the Russians thought it was their own troops, Jäger or others who wanted to take cover behind the line to regroup. For this reason they did not fire on them, remaining in perfect order [...] as soon as they saw the French masses, they threw them to the side exposing their cannons, hidden in their ranks, which unleashed a volley that upset all the Russian columns [...] at that moment we Austrians were also being attacked by the enemy, from all sides [...] in order to respond to the attack I moved my battalion forward, lined up en masse [...] As soon as that movement was over I noticed that the enemy was preparing a frontal attack. As soon as their movement began, I sent out a volley, forcing them to retreat. In the meantime Beaulieu's battalion, deployed on Kerpen's flank, was furiously attacked by French grenadiers and repulsed [...] I then attempted a counterattack with a Reuss-Greitz battalion; during this advance we suffered a severe fire that hit and wounded many soldiers, killed others together with Captain Nigel. Because of these losses and because my left flank was now threatened*

▲ *Eve of the Battle of Austerlitz*, Louis Albert Guislain Bacler d'Albe, 1808. According to historian Jacques Garnier, it was during these hours that Napoleon matured his strategy for the next day.

by the enemy, my battalion fell back. I urged them to stop [...] a few bursts of gunfire slowed down the enemy fire and made the transport of the wounded less dangerous. The Reuss-Greitz battalion, which was on my flank, also fell back [...] I had 2 captains and more than 100 wounded soldiers, plus one captain and 72 soldiers killed [...] so that my battalion, which had 312 men at the beginning of the hostilities, was left with only 80 soldiers."

Kutuzov still has his Guard at his disposal to attempt to retake Pratzen, so that the conquest of the high ground and the splitting of the enemy line in two are still not certain. The Russian Guard numbered 5500 soldiers and 2500 cavalry sabres, waiting near Krenowitz with the order to parade northwards, to Blasowitz, to support Liechtenstein's cavalry and protect Bagration's left. Hearing the cannonades on Pratzen, the Guard headed west to attack the left wing of Vandamme, deployed on Staré Vinohrady, a position occupied at 11 o'clock by the French. But the Russian Guard was already spotted by the 4th Line. *"At that moment, Captain Vincent, General Ferey's Aide-de-Camp, galloped towards the 1st Battalion of the 4th Line. Although he was not the bearer of a written order, he urges the Major to march forward to complete the defeat of the Russians and collect prisoners. The battalion climbs, at a charging pace, a slope covered with vineyards and fruit trees, from the crest of which they discover, in the distance, an enemy column beating a retreat. But soon, instead of a disorderly troop, seven battalions stand out in order, supported by as many squadrons, which retreat at a walking pace and form, as it were, the rear guard of the broken line."*

The episode is confirmed by Auguste Bigarré, an officer of the 4th Line, sent to reconnoiter a battalion, to understand who was coming: *"General Vandamme ordered me to put myself at the head of this battalion and to go and examine that column. He told his aide-de-camp, Vincent, to accompany me. I was about a quarter of a mile from my division, when Captain Vincent, who preceded my Eclaireurs, discovered on the slopes of a hill a considerable mass of cavalry. He came to me at a gallop and motioned me to make a conversion to "column head" to the left. I employed all the speed I could, to make that movement, continuing, however, to march in column, at section distance, to be ready for any eventuality and to make the square form. Once the direction was assigned to the battalion, led by its Chef-de-bataillon Guye, I, myself and with Captain Vincent, moved forward to see what was in that enemy column. As soon as we arrived on the plateau, which overlooked the two sides of the slope, we saw the enemy column advancing at a fast trot towards us. I returned, at breakneck speed, to my first battalion to square it off. That column, composed of all the cavalry of the Russian Imperial Guard, and commanded by Grand Duke Constantine, was formed on the plateau, at a long range of musketry from my battalion. It masked six pieces of light artillery, which, firing machine-gun fire on the battalion, succeeded in putting it in disorder."*

Napoleon left the command post on the Zuran, at 12 o'clock went up the Pratzen, and is together with Vandamme con-trolling the situation; he has brought with him part of the Imperial Guard, leaving Oudinot, on the plans of Turas, to possibly help Davout, if necessary. The Guard waits compactly, in absolute immobility, for the order to march. Amidst gusts of fog, which thins out, they see their own infantry on top of Pratzen. At that moment Napoleon orders the advance to Bessières. From his new command post, Bonaparte also orders Vandamme to head south in support of Saint-Hilaire, leaving the Staré to his Guard. Between the Guard and Oudinot's grenadiers, almost 11,000 bear-hair captains are in the field, and half of them climb to the pass, the hills: an impressive sight. Contrary to battle orders, Napoleon wanted to pay tribute to the two enemy emperors, present on the battlefield, by ordering that the bands remain in place, in the center of each battalion. Advancing, the Grenadiers sing a musical aria that is, for them, very familiar: *"On va leur percer le flan, Ran, ran, ran, tan plan tire lire. On va leur percer le flanc, Que nous allons rire. Ran tan plan tire lire, Que nous allons rire."* Music and drums mix in an exciting crescendo.

▲ The long line of French cuirassiers hides the movement of artillery behind it. By Jules Jacquet 1894.

While the positions are changing, the cavalry of the Russian Guard also arrives and falls on the 4th line and the 24th light of Vandamme, still stopped on the Staré Vinohrady, in the northern part. The French rout and run to their own brigades, backing away chaotically but saved by a counter charge from the French Imperial Guard cavalry. *"The battalion had continued its march while the enemy cavalry, seeing the isolation and weakness of that troop, turned and maneuvered to outflank it. The battalion commander formed a square, advancing in this formation: but obstacles of every kind disordered the platoons, and soon it was necessary to stop and reform the faces of the square. The Russian infantry, who had been observing these movements, threw their sacks on the ground and, with an abrupt reversal, threw themselves upon the first division. Greeted by a platoon fire, which soon turned, without command, into a chaotic and deadly fire at will, the Russians continued their movement, and, owing to their numerical superiority, overflowed from the wings.*

The Chef-de-bataillon made, then, maneuver his square. This unfortunate maneuver, brought the half-battalion si-nistra out of the vineyards and onto the ridge, offering it to the view of the machine-gun of three mouths of fire. Charged by the Russian cavalry, it was disbanded and its rout transmitted to the right platoons, which ran to retreat behind the 24th Light. In this chaos the flag bearer was mortally wounded and fell with his eagle. A non-commissioned officer, wanting to pick up the eagle, was, in turn, killed. A soldier took over and grabbed the eagle from the non-commissioned officer's hands, but he was, too, put out of action, unable to prevent Constantin's cavalry from removing their trophy." The Russian story is different (Hors série N°2 de Soldats Napoléoniens - octobre 2003) *"Russian Lieutenant Khmelev knocked down the eagle-carrier, whose flag fell to the ground, cuirassier Gavrilov, jumped off his horse, picked up the much coveted emblem and handed it to his comrade Omelchenko. For a moment a French furior took it back, but he was soon killed as well. A third non-commissioned officer, Sergeant Major Prevost Saint-Cyr managed to get hold of it but, literally taken by sabre rattling, he fell in turn. In the end, the Russians Omelchenko, Ushakov and Lasunov emerged victorious from this atrocious melee and carried the eagle of the first battalion to their leader, the Grand Duke Constantine".*

It is the 24th light regiment that has the worst of it. Instead of creating squares, it makes the mistake of facing the Russian cavalry in compact masses; the latter overwhelms them and sends them en route. Auguste Bigarré comments on the fact of the lost eagle: *"A non-commissioned officer of my 1st battalion had collected, on the battlefield, one of the eagles of the 24th light, believing it was the one lost by our battalion. So no one immediately noticed that it was missing from the roll call."*

Napoleon's Guard, as mentioned, in turn supported by the Drouet Division of Bernadotte's I Corps, is moving up the northern Pratzen to relieve Vandamme's proven units. Bernadotte's arrival, in practice, makes the French occupation of the Pratzen final and cuts the Coalition army in two.

After midday Kutuzov had no more reserve to oppose to the 11.500 men led by Bernadotte. The same Russian Guard is devastated by the cavalry shoulders of the Guard of Bessières and the Russians have only to retreat towards Krenowitz. The Austro-Russian center is definitively dismembered by Napoleon's ability to obtain numerical and tactical superiority in every key point of the battle, except for the northern part of the battlefield where the forces were equal. The few unforeseen and critical situations that occurred were brilliantly resolved by the Empereur's capacity for improvisation. Bernadotte's final dispatch against the Russian Guard is an example of this tactical sagacity.

As in Tellnitz, dangerous misunderstandings took place in the sector between Pratzen (Staré Vinohrady) and Holubitz, as told to us by Gervais, whose 13th Light Infantry advanced decisively: *"A sergeant of the 1st Carabineer Company (the elite light infantry company) of our regiment glanced at a battalion that seemed to have something strange in its march. He approached it and recognized it as a Russian battalion. So he warned our commander, who ordered a conversion of the front right, to oppose the march of that battalion. The Russian commander, seeing himself discovered, lowered his weapons.*

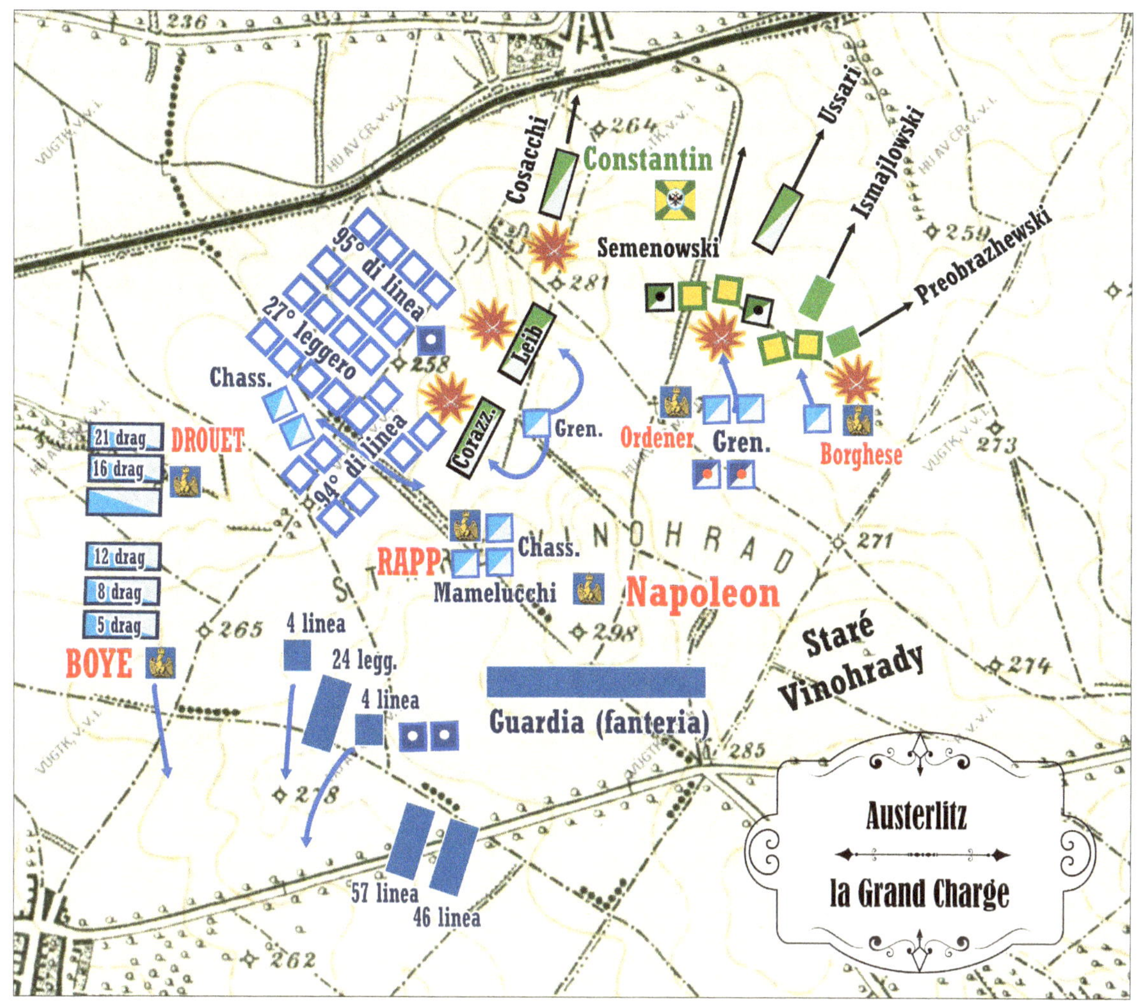

It was a battalion that, having been isolated, had separated from its own and hoped to escape by following our movements. At that time we could easily be deceived. The Russians had made considerable changes in their outfit at that time.

They still had green jackets, but much less long ones, than in 1799 in Zurich. Then, as we were in winter, they wore, like us, their coats over their clothes, and these were similar to ours ... We kept walking forward. The enemy was in retreat."

"Now it's the cavalry's turn," Bessières apparently exclaimed to his aide César de Laville. The rout of the 4th of the line and the 24th light triggered the episode that has gone down in history as the Grand Charge d'Austerlitz. Bessières activates the 42 mamelukes of the Guard of Honor, the mounted grenadiers under the command of Colonel Ordener (the "black horses" or also called "the invincibles") with a squadron commanded by Prince Borghese, Pauline Bonaparte's husband. This is how Grenadier Coignet describes the Mamelukes: "L'Empereur made us stop, throwing forward the Mamelukes and the chasseurs à cheval. Those mamelukes were exceptional horsemen, they did what they wanted with their horse. With their curved saber, they cut off a head with one blow, and with their sharp stirrups they opened the kidneys of the soldiers. One of them went back three times to bring the Emperor a Russian flag, Napoleon wanted to stop by him but that one left again, and did not return. He fell on the battlefield."

▲ French troops array themselves at Austerlitz (reenactors in French uniforms). Courtesy by Keith Redfern.

The Russian cavalry attempts to reverse the situation, bringing in a column of cavalry on the right with Prince Liechtenstein at the head. The Russian cavalry attacks the center of Vandamme's division. Napoleon follows the event on the hill of the old vineyards (Staré Vinohrady). When Napoleon launches his Ordener "black horses" the first charge is wobbling. Recounts Grenadier on foot Jean-Roch Coignet: *"The Russian Imperial Guard was made up of gigantic men who fought to the extreme. Our cavalry was all in disarray. Then the Empereur launched the 'black horses', that is, the mounted grenadiers ... they passed us by some thunderbolts and sank into the enemy ranks. For a quarter of an hour there was an impressive melee, that quarter of an hour seemed like a century!"*

Noon has recently passed. Two French regiments are fighting a vain battle against the cavalry of the Russian guard. The first charge sent by Napoleon himself (the one with the mounted grenadiers and the Mamelukes) also comes down against the machine-gun fire of the Russian guns. Some horsemen enter the Russian formation, but are immediately repelled. Then starts the second wave of the Chasseurs under the command of Colonel Morland (will fall on the battlefield, will be embalmed by Larrey and sent to Paris in a barrel of rum. They say that when the barrel was opened his hair and moustache reached his feet). Napoleon then orders his aide-de-camp, General Rapp, to lead a second attack with the Chasseurs à Cheval. This attack was more successful and the Russian Guard, this time, was forced to retreat, leaving behind many dead and wounded. It was a terrible fight between elite units, which will not influence the outcome of the battle, but will go down in history.

Bessières, who wanted to spare the soldiers of the Guard as much as possible, did not employ all of his forces. The first wave, therefore, was controlled and repulsed by the Russian grenadier regiment Semenovski, but the artillery of the Guard of Doguereu intervened and began to beat mercilessly the infantry of the Archduke Constantine. The second wave of charge involved Ordener, in command of the last squadron of mounted grenadiers, flanked by two squadrons of Chasseurs led by Dahlmann and with Borghese still on the right. At the same time General Drouet advances his regiments and unloads his muskets, first on the flank of the Cossacks of the Guard and then on the Russian infantry that is divided in half. The French cavalry repaired behind the friendly squares to reorganize and to start a third wave against the Semenovski and Prebrazhenski regiments. It is the final act of the fight on Pratzen, the Russian Guard leaves on the ground 500 soldiers, the prince Repnin, commander of a squadron of the Russian Leib Guard is taken, with its 200 horsemen; the rest fall back on Krenovitz in disorder. At about 1 o'clock the Austro-Russian center is retreating, and the southern part of the theater is in serious trouble, with the French also behind.

THE "QUIET" FRONT IN THE NORTH AND THE END OF THE BATTLE IN THE SOUTH

In the north the morning had been less dense with important events. The Russians had deployed the Guard (which would later move up to the Pratzen) behind the village of Blasowitz, sending one of their vanguards to occupy it. The center of the sector is occupied by the Austro-Russian cavalry of the Prince of Liechtenstein, the one that had mistaken the initial deployment; the Russian vanguard of Bagration, almost an army corps, is on the right, in front of Kowalowitz.

The Prince of Liechtenstein, who has just finished deploying between Krug and Holubitz, opens the hostilities. His troops are still moving when General Essen starts the charge, perhaps too early, leading the Ulans of the Imperial Guard, aiming at Kellerman's cavalry, which is the advanced center of the French deployment. The first violent charge is repulsed and the Ulans regroup. Essen II then turns his cavalry against Caffarelli's infantry, riding alongside Suchet's 34th line regiment; all the French are already in square formation, some not even forming it. Galloping towards Caffarelli, the Ulans suffer the 34th regiment's rifle fire on their flank and are decimated, losing ¼ of their strength in wounded and dead. The 51st French Line tells the story: *"The Ulans, launched at a gallop, could not find our light cavalry, finding, in their place, a firm line of infantry, which welcomed them with a deadly musketry fire. Several platoons, however, entered the line and were greeted by the 51st infantry that, without even forming a square, fired at will: 400 of those horsemen remained on the ground. Taking advantage of the incident, Kellermann, charges the remains of Grand Duke Constantin's regiment, passing a large number of them by saber. Prince Johann Lichtenstein is forced to send part of his squadrons to rescue the Ulans."*

Artilleryman Levavasseur relates Kellermann's charge: *"Kellermann's cavalry makes a movement of four, turns to the left, and defiles; but, as our infantry does not let it pass, it gallops along the line, in order to penetrate through the intervals. All the cavalry of the Grand Duke Constantine rushes against our pieces; the soldiers throw themselves under the caissons and under the cannon; the artillerymen throw themselves with their sticks; our infantry cannot fire, finding themselves covered by the mass of Kellermann's cavallery. But soon after, the line opens and makes a beating fire, thirty paces on the enemy. I was then encased between my draft horses, fighting hand-to-hand with an officer, who had already taken away the little finger of my right hand, with a saber blow, when that officer's horse collapsed struck by a bullet. The officer rushed to my stirrup and yelled, "Admit it, we're brave."* (Editor's note: almost all Russian officers at the time spoke French).

Kellermann then counter-charged, but his 4th Hussars were surrounded and blocked; the French did not give up, charged again and freed the captive Hussars, forcing the Russian Ulans to retreat to regroup behind Blasowitz. In the action they capture Russian General Miller-Zakomelski while General Essen II is mortally wounded. Kutuzov meanwhile called for Hohenlohe's support on the Starè Vinohrady, against the 4th of the line; the Austrian charge, however, is blocked by the vineyards and has no effect.

▲ The Pratzen as seen from the French cannon line. Courtesy by John Callahan.

As for the French, Marshal Lannes arranged his infantry to the north (Suchet) in two lines, the first consisting of bat-taglions in formation, the second in columns deployed behind the intervals. At 8 a.m. Prince Bagration planned to cut off the Suchet division, striking its left and bypassing the Santon, along the Bosenitz crevasse. Hearing the roar of cannons to the south Bagration notes, *"I don't see why I should stand here, idle, watching the enemy move reinforcements from his left wing to his right wing."* Bagration is an aggressive commander and around 9 o'clock, continuing to hear the roar of battle to the south, he orders the advance. He deployed his infantry in the center in two lines under the command of Prince Piotr Dolgoruki. The 6th Jäger Regiment is at Holubitz and Kruh, supported by the Cossacks of Kiseljev, Malakov, and Kaznhekov. Adjutant General Fiodor Uvarov is put on the left wing, with the Hussars of Elisavetgrad, the Dragoons of Chernigov and Kharkov, while Bagration assembles ten squadrons of Hussars from Mariupol and Pavlograd as the right wing. Prince Piotr also forms a reserve (under the command of Major General Efim Chaplitz and Piotr Wittgenstein, which included Her Majesty the Czarina's Cuirassiers of the Guard (Leib), Ulans of the Guard, and St. Petersburg Dragoons. In total, Bagration has about 14000 men, supported by 30 cannons, almost all of them battalion (light). Moreover, the Prince of Liechtenstein deploys his 4600 cavalrymen to cover the kilometer and a half that separates the north wing and the center on the Staré Vinohrady. At 9.30 the two adversaries clash. General Claparède maintains his strong entrenched position and, on the left of the Santon, Bagration is pushed back by the line infantry regiments, 24th and 40th. The threat of being taken on the flank by the Caffarelli division causes Bagration to retreat and suggests that Suchet resume a vigorous advance that leads him to occupy the Old Post Station at Posoritz.

Lannes deployed the Caffarelli division on his right, in connection with the forces of Vandamme on Pratzen and, at 10.30 sent it to attack Blasowitz, occupied by a battalion of the Russian Guard

(Semenovsky) and by the Hunters of the Guard commanded by a French emigré, Saint-Priest. Caffarelli sends forward the 13th Light preceded by four companies of Tirailleurs with, on his right, the 51st Line. The 51st Line remembers: *"It must have been 11 o'clock in the morning, the Caffarelli and Suchet divisions, momentarily rid of the squadrons of the Prince of Lichtenstein, advance to attack the village of Blasowitz; despite being exposed to the terrible fire of 22 artillery pieces, they march with resolute step. The musicians who, by order of Napoleon, remain in the center of the battalions, play, with drums beating the charge"*.

At the head of the II battalion of the 13th light, Colonel Castex attacks the village and dies in the assault; it is a French victory with the capture of about 200 prisoners. The flanking action of the 51st line leads to the capture of another 250 Russian Guards, while Kellermann sends his cavalry to capture the cannon battery in position in front of the village.

Etienne Gervais, rifleman of the 13th Light Brigade, tells us about those anguished moments: *"Having taken the village, we made a new forward movement. We arrived at a small, shallow valley where the enemy occupied the slope opposite to that from which we were arriving. There, we stopped and the Russian artillery hit us again. We were still, given the distance, unable to respond to that fire. Our artillery, positioned between the intervals of our battalions, was also firing heavily. We could see enemy cavalry approaching our center, preparing to charge us. I, as a rifleman, was guarding the flag, in the front row, on the left. A ball had hit my bayonet and twisted it horizontally, so that it was useless for defense. This worried me, especially in case of a cavalry charge, which did not seem to be delayed ... Of 51, which was on our left, many men had fallen, whose rifles were on the ground. To avoid leaving my first line and crossing the other two, I begged one of my friends, Renier, quartermaster of the fourth*

▲ Map of the Austerlitz campaign.

▲ The return of the Russian cuirassiers after the battle. Canvas by Nikolai-Samokish.

company, to pass me one of these rifles. Renier took two or three steps; then, returning to his seat, he said to me, "If you want a rifle, take it yourself. The balls fall too hard. If I am to be killed, I want to be killed in my place." I left my rank to get the rifle. I had not passed completely behind the standard-bearer, that a ball killed the two men in the line, whom I had just left, my friend Renier, and the other, named Charpentier, furior of the seventh. If I had stayed in my place, two seconds longer, I would have been the first to die, because I was in the first row. I reamed a rifle on the fly (sic); I made sure of its condition, that of the bayonet, then returned to my row."

With the occupation of Blasowitz completed, Murat brought forward Nansouty's heavy cavalry, sent it charging against the Austro-Russian front line, which with the Carabinieri created the gap; the second line was forced by the Corazzieri who pushed the Austro-Russians over the Holubitz Bridge. According to the account of the 51st Line: *"The enemy, in force, had suddenly emerged from the village (Blasowitz) to try to surround the Caffarelli division on the right; but the latter, wanting to prevent the mano-vra, opposed them the 51st and the 13th light. After a lively fight, the 51st took 400 prisoners and the village of Blasowitz remained in our power. Once Blasowitz is taken, Lannes occupies Holubitz and Kruh, villages located along the road to Olmütz, and comes into contact with Bagration's infantry. He brings the Suchet division obliquely to the left and the Caffarelli division obliquely to the right. With this divergent movement, Lannes separates Bagration's infantry from the cavalry of the Prince of Lichtenstein, pushing the former back to the right of the Olmütz road, the latter to the right, towards the ascent to the Pratzen heights. At that moment the cavalry will make a second attempt, plunging entirely against the Caffarelli division, formed on a single line, which will receive the charge with cold blood and abundant musketry. Lichtenstein's numerous squadrons, though in disorder, are realigned and thrown a second time against our battalions. This time the Cuirassiers of Nansouty and d'Hautpoul, who were standing behind Caffarelli's infantry, intervene, defile at a trot behind the ranks of the infantry, deploy on his right, and send the formidable mass of enemy cavalry en route."*

At those junctures, Lannes is informed of the success of the advance on the Pratzen. He ordered a general attack by his infantry. He moves Suchet's troops toward Kowalowitz and Caffarelli's division toward Holubitz, while the rest of his infantry and cavalry of Kellermann and Walther fight Bagration along the major road. Caffarelli's troops face stubborn resistance from Bagration's 6th Jäger at Holubitz before driving him from the houses.

At 11 o'clock Kutuzov recalls Archduke Constantine and the Russian Guard on Pratzen to try to counterattack Vandamme's French; the departure of the Tsarist elite force weakens the entire central line, now held only by Lie-chtenstein's units. The situation between the northern and central sectors seems confused. Bagration, meanwhile, has deployed his forces along the Olmütz road with three infantry regiments across the road with cavalry on the flanks. He directs the 5th Jäger regiment, supported by Mariupol's hussars and Khaznekov's Cossacks, to the heights near Siwitz. Prince Peter wants to make an encircling movement on the French left flank, while his main forces attack Lannes in front.

The 5th Jäger pushed into the French positions, as far as Siwitz, and then attempted to reach Bosenitz and the Santon. According to an official Austrian report, *"The French outposts were over-thrown in a short time, and only artillery fire from the [French] left wing there above [Santon] pre-vented the fugitives from being completely wiped out by the Cossacks and Mariupol hussars, who came running. Jäger and Cossacks pushed into Bosenitz itself and surprised a crowd of marauders, some of whom were brought back as prisoners, and the rest were executed on the spot."* A battalion of the French 17th Light withdrew in order, repelling Russian charges, to the Santon, where the French bat-tery bombarded the Russians, forcing them to retreat. Observing the 5th Jäger retreating, the 2nd bat-talion of the 17th light, counterattacks and, supported by the cavalry, reconquers Bosenitz. Seeing the crisis in the central part of the battlefield, Bagration takes the initiative and tries to move towards the right in order to threaten the Santon pass. The Russian Jäger, followed by the Cossacks and the Mariupol hussars, entered Bosenitz, but were repulsed by the cavalry of Milhaud and Treilhard and by the 88th line regiment.

General Suchet took advantage of this to advance his troops in line, against the deployed lines of Bagration. After securing the flanks, Lannes, resumes his general advance. Bagration fights the French with the salvoes of his batteries and the Russian artillery fire is so effective that, in a few minutes, Lannes' troops lose about 400 men, including dead and wounded.

It is at this point of the battle that General Valhubert has a leg taken off by a cannonball that devastates his thigh. He refuses to be evacuated and almost dies on the field, bleeding out (in reality he will be taken to Brno, where he died and his tomb is today a tourist destination). The advance of Suchet is supported by the charges of Kellermann to north of Kruh; also this general takes a ball that smashes his leg, as is wounded also the brigadier Walther that charges with his Dragoons. Eventu-ally Bagration's entire line is pushed back beyond Kowalowitz.

The French put in position about fifteen cannons and in fact silenced Bagration's fire mouths. At the same time, Lannes orders the 30th and 17th line regiments to proceed along the left flank to rein-force Suchet. Bagration now faces Suchet's and Caffarelli's infantry divisions, supported by Murat's Reserve cavalry. French light cavalry pursued the remnants of the 5th Jäger Regiment and Mariupol's hussars on the left flank, while the forces of d'Hautpoul, Kellermann, and Walther massed in the center and on the right flank.

Despite the French superiority, Bagration's infantry resisted by inflicting significant losses. Suchet comments: *"Deployed in lines, our infantry resisted the incessant fire with total composure, filling the ranks as soon as they had gaps. The second line suffered greatly from the [Russian] artillery, but remained impassive."*

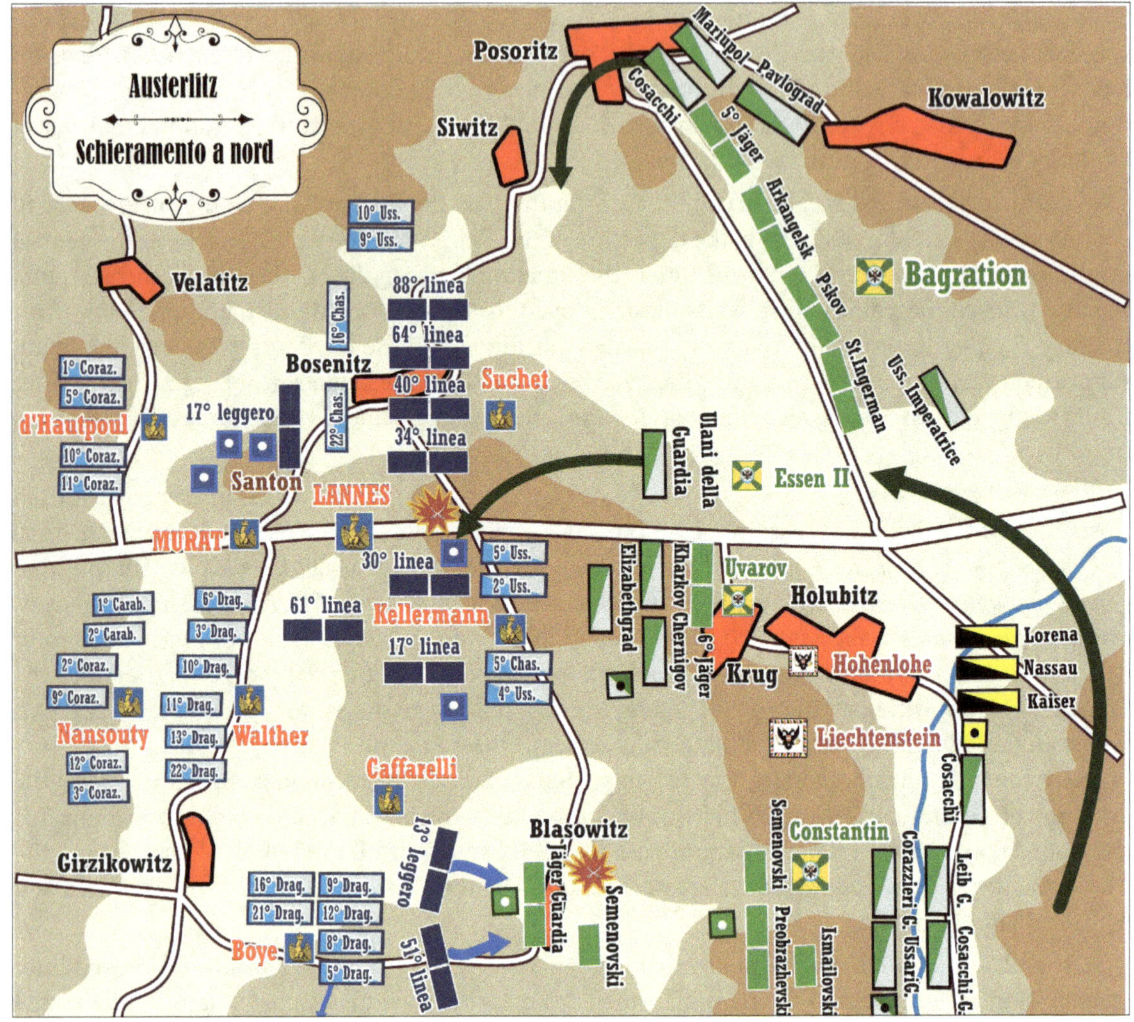

It was already afternoon when Lannes finally secured the villages of Holubitz and Kruh and finally pushed Bagration's forces along the major road. To the north, General d'Hautpoul engages the 5th Jäger, retreating from Siwitz to Posorsitz, and then to Kowalowitz. Bagration has not received any orders or messages, during the battle, but in the afternoon they will report to him the collapse of the Russian center and left flank.

The last pockets of Russian resistance ceased fighting under the blows of d'Hautpoul's heavy cavalry, and by 3 p.m. the entire plateau north of Holubitz was cleared of Austro-Russians, with Bagration retreating.

Bagration took advantage of the brief truce, followed by the shift of events to the south, to gather his troops and withdrew in the direction of Raussnitz, where he arrived shortly after 16.00. Murat stopped his advance at 17.30 when he received the news that Krenowitz, beyond Pratzen, was occupied by Bernadotte's corps, thinking that Napoleon might still need his cavalry to the south. In the end, the only formation still able to fight was Bagration's column. Tsar Alexander ordered the remnants of his army to march to Hungary and Prince Piotr to cover the retreat.

Having secured control of Pratzen and realizing that on the northern front Bagration had drifted eastward, becoming a harmless force, Napoleon then turned his attention to the southern end of the battlefield, where the French and Allies were still fighting for possession of Sokolnitz and Tellnitz. Bernadotte's I Corps, which until then had not contributed much to the battle, was ordered to hold the Pratzen plateau and move on to Krenowitz, while the task of launching a new attack was still entrusted to the tried units of Saint-Hilaire and Vandamme, supported by Legrand's 3rd Division and Davout, who had to liberate Sokolnitz. The assault is developed on two fronts: the Saint-Hilaire division, with part of the 3rd corps of Davout and with general Legrand on his right, breaks through the enemy defenses in Sokolnitz, capturing, they say, 4000 prisoners and forcing the commanders of the first two allied columns, generals Michael von Kienmayer and Langéron, to flee as quickly as possible towards the south, after the useless resistance. In the meantime Vandamme marches on the southern edge of the Pratzen, where he presses Buxhöwden's line.

At 14, while Kutuzov studies the directives for the retreat, (the Tsar and the whole General Staff had already left an hour earlier), his center, Kollowrath, the Russian Guard and Liechtenstein cavalry, which has left Holubitz, appears, if not en route, in harried retreat to the east. The battle is over and the Allied army has been practically destroyed. Allied headquarters is in total chaos. Prince Czartoriski describes a total confusion among the senior Russian officers and sees General Buxhöwden, who: *"had lost his hat and his clothes were in disarray; when he saw me at a distance, he shouted: They have abandoned me! They have sacrificed me!"*

At 3:30 p.m. Krenowitz fell; in the south many Russian soldiers no longer listened to the officers and began a disorderly escape, fearing being surrounded. Grenadier Coignet, from the chapel of St. Anthony notes, *"All the troops clapped their hands, and our Napoleon devoted himself to his snuffbox; it was the total defeat of the enemy. Then, in the midst of these solemn circumstances, we found a way to laugh like boys. A hare, fleeing in fear, came straight to us. My captain Renard (Renard means fox in French) saw him and made a leap to "saber" him, but the hare made a dash for it. My captain continues to chase it and the poor animal has only time to take refuge, like a rabbit, in a hole. Those of us watching this hunt began to laughingly shout, "The fox won't catch the hare! The fox won't catch the hare!" And indeed he failed to catch it; nay, he laughed at himself, so excellent a man was the captain, esteemed and beloved of all his soldiers."*

▲ The hasty and disorderly course of the Russians at the end of the battle. Canvas by Nikolai-Samokish

The Coalition army, tired and demoralized, with a few hints of panic, falls back in long columns towards the east. Some fall back passing over the frozen ponds of Mönitz and Satschan. They narrate that the French artillery, from the chapel of Saint Anthony, bombarded them, breaking the ice of the ponds, thus causing many deaths by drowning. This af-firmation is exaggerated because the distance between the chapel and the ponds was out of range of the French artillery of the time. In reality, all the artillery on the Pratzen is on the move, and the drains made by the Moravians in later eras will belie this historical footnote. According to other sources, it is said that after the draining of the basin, several dozen corpses of horses and some cannons were found, but only two or three bodies of Russian soldiers. Only legends.

At past sixteen o'clock the night comes and, like a theatrical curtain, closes this act of the Napoleonic wars. *"I have seen many battles lost, but I never thought of such a defeat!"* wrote Russian General Langeron in his notes.

Among the ranks of the Allied army there was no man who knew this location better than the commander of the Austro-Russian cavalry, Count Johann I of Liechtenstein; he owned, at the time, the entire Posoritz estate. Besides Johann of Liechtenstein, there was also his cousin Johann Baptist Joseph Möritz who commanded a mixed cavalry brigade in the southern vanguard of Kienmayer. It will be just Johann to be sent by the Austrian Emperor Franz II, to Napoleon with the proposal of capitulation. It is almost dawn of December 3, when the French emperor, satisfied, lies down on a haystack and falls asleep, exhausted. But the sleep will not last long. Johann von Liechtenstein arrives at the Old Post Station, the battle over. After some hesitation Napoleon's aide-de-camp wakes him up, with the following words, *"Baron Liechtenstein is here."* Napoleon listens to the Austrian diplomat and receives the capitulation: *"Your Excellency has nothing more to conquer,"* says Liechtenstein, *"the battle is so defined that you cannot add anything more. Only peace can be added."*

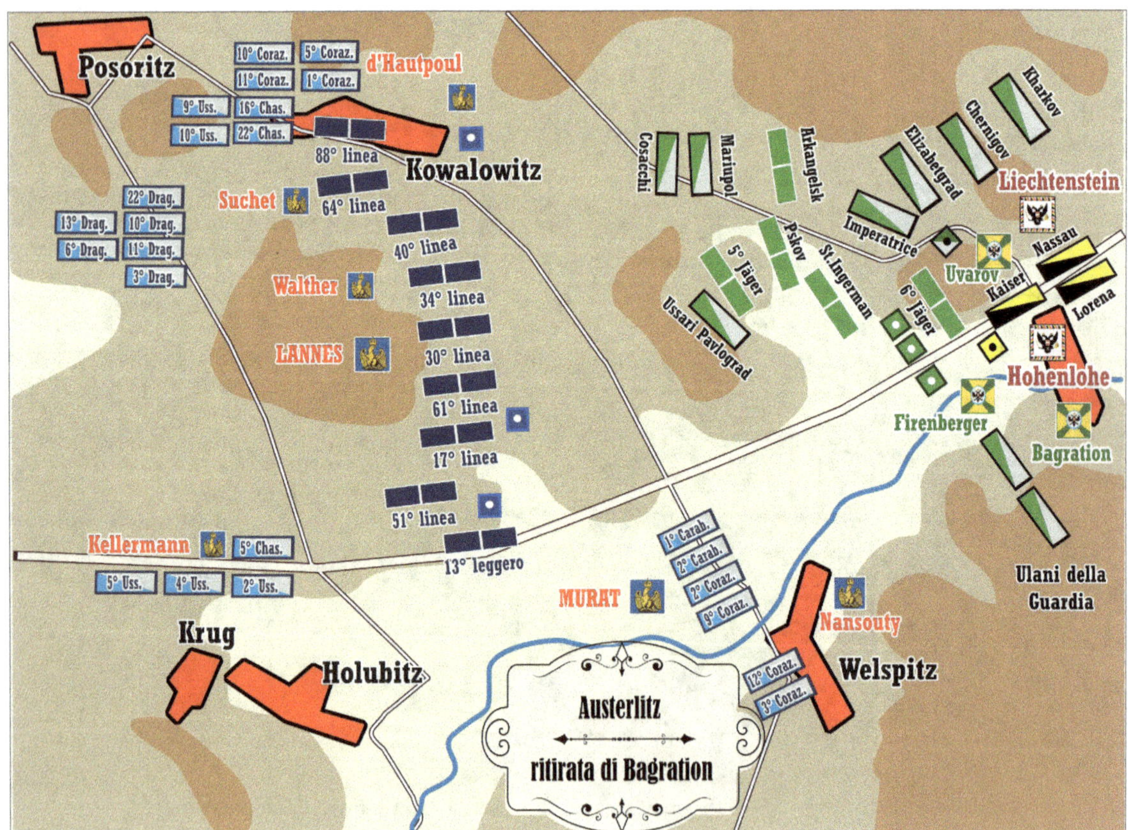

THE LOSSES

The French at Austerlitz lost 1537 dead and had 7000 wounded. The Russians lost 21000 men dead, wounded and missing plus 133 artillery pieces (justified by the muddy and uneven terrain), the Austrians 5922. The number of Russians is impressive, but it must be said that many of them had escaped, traveling through Moravia and Silesia, to finally make their way home. The Russians also lost 9767 prisoners, the Austrians 1686 and the French only 573. It should be noted that the number of French dead is much higher than the one transmitted by Napoleon, after the battle (this also takes into account the dead in the days following the battle, since on the day of the battle 884 soldiers and 69 officers died on the field) and that 79% of the losses were borne by the infantry. The youngest French soldier who died at Austerlitz, Ciarre, was 15 years old and was a member of the Tirailleurs battalion, a unit that also had the oldest soldier to die, Germolacci.

The most famous fallen of Austerlitz was certainly the defender of the Santon, Brigadier General Valhubert. They say that an hour before his death he wrote to Napoleon: *"I would have liked to do more for you; I will die soon. I do not regret life at all, because I have been part of a victory that will make you a happy Kingdom. When You think of the brave men who have been devoted to You, think of my memory. It is enough for me to tell You that I have a family; I have no need to recommend them to You."* Jean Marie Roger Valhubert, would die in Brno and be buried in the city's former cemetery. The tombstone of the highest officer, who died in battle, can be found today in the Tyrš Park in Brno,

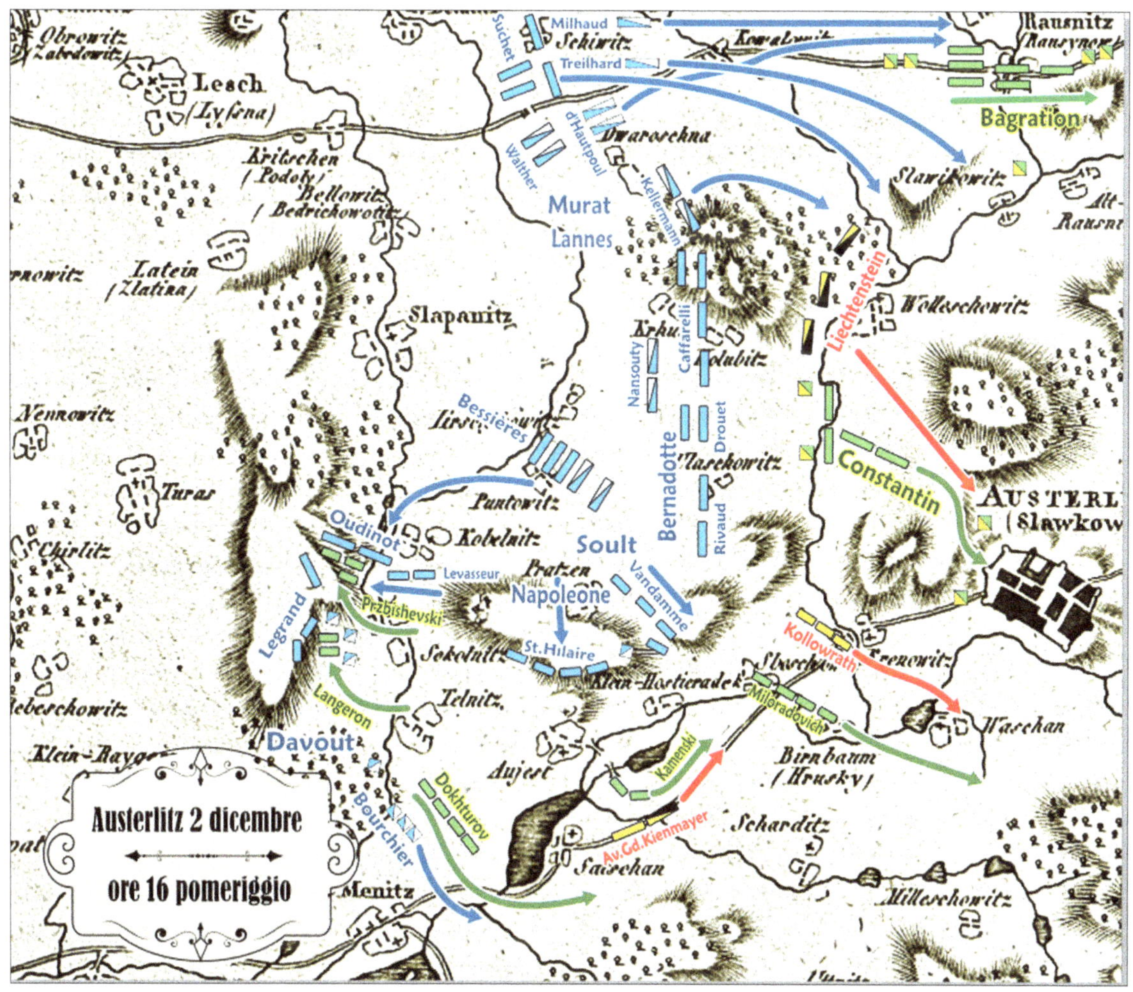

▲ A coeval image of the battle.

between Kounicova Street and Botanická Street, so not far from the city center. Valhubert, on the Santon, was mortally wounded, hit by a cannonball or the burst of a grenade. He was truly a man with the vocation of a hero. When his soldiers wanted to help him, he rebuked them with the following words: *"Go back to your positions, I can die here too. It is not necessary for one man to lose six others!"* Despite the general's insistence, his soldiers transported him to the lazaret of Šlapanice and from there to Brno, where he died three days later. The funeral ceremony took place in the church of St. James. After the mass, the soldiers carried his mortal remains on their shoulders to the cemetery.

In Brno, near the Old Marketplace, there is still the Reduta Theater, probably the oldest theater building in Central Europe. The French took Russian prisoners there after the Battle of Austerlitz. Shortly afterwards, a hospital for unsportable wounded of the French army was installed there. Other wounded remained in lazarettos around the Austerlitz battlefield, such as at Šlapanice or Ponětovice. One of those transported to Brno, was General Thiébault, who was seriously wounded. He was being carried on a stretcher by four Russian soldiers, when six Frenchmen abruptly replaced them, saying, *"It is up to us to carry a French general."* The blow, which had gone through his body, had also generated numerous internal injuries and seven fractures. No one thought he would survive. Having a presentiment of his imminent end, Napoleon himself pronounced a brief eulogy: *"You cannot have a more beautiful death,"* he told his general, who certainly touched iron. Thanks to the excellent work of the doctors, however, the general made a miraculous recovery. However, this irritated Kajetán Unterweeger, the guardian of the printing shop in Orlí Street, where the general was convalescing. The general had his own personal surgeon, his own valet, his own cook, three servants, fourteen horses and eight escort men. He occupied six rooms, which Unterweeger had to heat. *"God be with me!"* said the poor guar-dian, *"I do not know what I shall yet have to provide and procure."*

Besides the lucky Thiébault, other officers had a hard time at Austerlitz. The Count of Saint-Hilaire was wounded at the beginning of the attack on Pratzen and remained all day on the battlefield, inciting his troops. The general of division Kellermann, the count Walther, the generals of brigade count Sébastiani, Dumont, Manzy, the counts Compans and Rapp, aides de camp of the emperor, remained all wounded. Rapp, charging at the head of the Grenadiers of the Guard, captured the Russian prince Repnin, commander of the cavalry of the Russian Imperial Guard. The French Guard, on the other hand, lost the colonel of the chasseurs à cheval, Morland, who was blown to pieces by machine gunfire while charging a battery of Russian Guard cannons. Colonel Mazas, of the 14th Line, was killed, while Colonel Corbineau, squire of the Empress, commander of the 5th regiment of chasseurs à cheval, had four horses killed while he was riding them and, on the fifth, was wounded while capturing an enemy flag.

As for the treatment of the wounded, it is interesting to note the case of Schlapanitz or Lapanz (today Šlapanice). During the battle of Austerlitz, the village was located in the immediate French rearguard, which made it an ideal place for the treatment of the wounded but also for the detention of prisoners. During the battle, about 400 Russians were detained in the church. Two large buildings served the needs of the military doctors - the old monastic schools (now a museum) and the Blümegen Castle, where field hospitals and a surgical unit were installed. At the time of the battle, Jean Dominique Larrey, chief surgeon of the French Imperial Guard, went to work there. Larrey was known for introducing new and, in some ways, revolutionary protocols in treating the sick. The first thing was a real innovation for the time: it was to provide the first rudimentary care as quickly as possible, a kind of pre-medication. For this they used mobile ambulances on wagons, called "flying ambulances" (ambulances because they were mobile). This was a real revolution in the medical field (hence the idea of First Aid) since, until then, even the wounded with the most serious injuries remained on the battlefield, often for many hours, without any help. Despite the great shortage of medical equipment and poor hygienic conditions, Larrey and his assistants saved dozens of lives,

▲ The Battle of Austerlitz in December 1805 at 4 p.m., canvas by Jean Antoine Simeon Fort.

thanks to timely and well-executed interventions.

Surgical care did not have many options at the time. The most frequent interventions were limb amputations, sometimes for minor wounds, to prevent gangrene of the infected wound. A circumscribed amputation took, for an experienced physician such as Larrey and his colleagues, incredibly only two to four minutes. The speed was necessary precisely because anesthesia did not yet exist . Larrey achieved a pseudo-anesthetic effect, through hypothermia of the wound or tincture of opium (laudanum). The wounded was, also, and often, drugged with aquavit. The only hopeless struggle was against epidemics of infectious diseases, which spread due to lack of proper hygiene.

"Never had a battlefield presented such an agonizing devastation as that of Austerlitz; the ground was covered with dead, dying, wounded, countless debris, weapons and armor, all sorts of objects scattered here and there, abandoned by the Russians since the first moments of the battle ... I returned at 4 a.m. to our central ambulance (a mill near Schlapanitz. Ed.) where we still gave medication to those who could not receive first aid. The next day I evacuated them all to Brün (Brno), accompanied by Surgeon Major Paulet, to be admitted to the convent used as a hospital ... His Majesty also gave me the task of collecting and preserving the body of the colonel of the chasseurs à cheval Morlan (Morland, who was later embalmed before being transferred to France, according to military custom), who had fallen in the first charge.

[...] We had just gathered, in the city of Brun, the French and Russian wounded, whose number was considerable, when an epidemic disease broke out among them, which we diagnosed as a putrid fever, nervous, malignant, nosocomial (adynamic - ataxic) or contagious typhus, as it was once called. It began with headaches, irregular chills, especially in the extremities. These chills were followed by a transient heat stroke. The sores, the suppuration of which diminished at first, assumed the character of hospital gangrene, which then made rapid progress. The pain in the head, external heat, and anxiety increased; the pulse, which had previously been weak and slow, became more intense and irregular; the urine was turbid and yellowish. In some subjects, the stool was normal; but in the greater number, diarrhea was one of the first symptoms of the disease. Hearing and sight acquired extreme sensitivity; the functions of the muscular system were disturbed; there was trembling in the limbs, trembling in the tendons, and co-munally delirium took possession of the sufferer at the end of this first period.

These first incidents were followed by pains in the epigastric region, colic, vomiting preceded and accompanied by hiccups ... The patient fell into sleep and into a state of general insensibility; he made automatic movements, of short duration, due to the prostration of forces. The pulse decreased in volume as it increased in speed; ... Whenever I saw this sign in the first period, I foresaw the fatal outcome of the disease [...] It was an epidemic. In fact, the sick in the same room were not slow to be affected by the same symptoms. The disease spread from neighbor to neighbor; it infected the hospitals, and subsequently the neighboring houses, because of the frequent communication of the individuals, and perhaps the transmission of the deleterious miasms, with the southern winds, when above all there was a very short distance to travel." Dominique-Jean Larrey, Chief Surgeon of the Guard.

That unknown disease, probably a bacterial infection or contagious typhus, was the real cause of the high mortality recorded after the battle. Hospitals were soon congested with feverish patients, and mortality increased proportionately. The epidemic also spread, at the same time, among the Russian prisoners, who had been crowded, in great numbers, into the churches and other capacious places; finally it was not long before it spread among the inhabitants, and subsequently extended over the whole line of evacuation, as far as France, by the effect of the transportation of the sick of the two nations and that of the prisoners.

THE EPILOGUE OF THE BATTLE

Why was it called like that? When Napoleon laid down his sword and picked up his pen to devote himself to reporting, his thoughts revolved around what to name the battle. How to baptize a battle that had taken place within a 120-square-kilometer radius, not far from Pratzen, Bosenitz, Tellnitz, Schlapanitz and many other villages? *"In all these places and at the same time? That's impossible. I have to come up with a majestic name,"* thought Napoleon surely. After a brief hesitation perhaps he wrote: *"I have found it!"*. Even though the battlefield extended further in front of Brno, the Battle of Brünn sounded bad in French. So the emperor named the battle after the place of his present residence, right there where he was with his Staff and it was *"the battle of Austerlitz"*. During the evening hours Napoleon pronounced his first proclamation from the balcony of the castle (the palace) to his soldiers, ending with the following words: *"Soldiers, when all that is necessary to ensure the happiness and prosperity of our country is accomplished, I will take you back to France; there you will be the object of my most tender solicitude. My people will see you again with joy, and it will be enough for you to say: - I was at the battle of Austerlitz - for them to reply, Here is a hero".*

This is all Napoleon. He knew the high currencies and propagandists well. But he was not too fond of concrete statistical facts. He often declared more victims on the side of the enemies than in reality. The French emperor knew how to make his victories described on paper look great. Near Austerlitz the armistice with Austria was also signed. On a rainy day, December 4, 1805. Napoleon was the first to arrive at the agreed upon location. *"Light two fires and pitch the tent,"* he ordered his soldiers. After a long wait Franz II arrived, who was certainly not in too much of a hurry considering how things had gone. He was together with Johann I of Liechtenstein, official escort of the Austrian emperor. Napoleon went towards the doors of Franz II's carriage saying *"I apologize but they are palaces that Your Excellency is forcing me to live in for two months"* and pointed to the tent near the road. Franz replied, eyewitnesses stated, *"You are very well in these mansions, Sir, so there is no reason to be angry."*

> The old mill on the burnt stream (Spálený Potok) between Žarošice and Násedlovice, known as "Spáleňák" became the silent testimon of another important event. Napoleon and Franz II agreed to an armistice under a linden tree that stood right there. The "historical" tree then listened to the dialogue in which the French emperor presented, to his opponent, the unpleasant account of his triumph.

▲ The old "burnt mill" building with the December 4 armistice plaque.

But why did the interview take place under a linden tree? In the original concerted plan, the confrontation of the two emperors was to take place inside the mill, but there was an unbearable stench, which added to the lack of space, forced them to change their plans. In the end, the negotiations took place under the branches of a linden tree, which was nearby. They conducted their talks in fours. On one side was Franz II, with the Prince of Liechtenstein, and on the other Napoleon, with Marshal Berthier. The emperors walked back and forth under the linden tree and stopped occasionally by the fire to warm up a bit. The officers of the two Sovereigns kept a polite distance and clustered around the second fire. *"That's too bad, because then we heard almost nothing,"* they said. In fact, no account of that conversation remained, except that the two Emperors were, probably, in good spirits. Towards the end Napoleon said, *"So, Your Excellency promises not to wage any more war against me?"* *"I swear it and I will keep my word,"* replied Franz II, who would deny himself four years later.

From then on people began to call that memorable linden tree, as "the imperial linden tree". A little later the Janův Dvůr (John's Court) was built, from which a small paved path led to the tree. One hundred years after the meeting of the emperors, in 1905, an information plaque with a bilingual, Czech-German inscription was placed on the facade of the court. *"Two days after the battle of Austerlitz, on December 4, 1805, the emperors Franz II and Napoleon met under the linden tree across the street to agree on an armistice and end that bloody war."* But with the passage of time the linden tree, to which no one had paid much attention, remained nothing but a rotten trunk. In 1919, a younger brother of the imperial lime tree was planted at the site of the historic meeting, and today it has become a very tall tree. For those interested, parts of the legendary trunk have been preserved and can be seen at Austerlitz Castle and at the Vrbas Museum in Ždánice Castle, where a whole section is dedicated to the Napoleonic theme.

Austerlitz Castle not only witnessed the repose of important Sovereigns, but also remarkable historical events. Although the terms of the armistice were sketched out at the mill, by Napoleon with Austrian Emperor Franz II, the actual signing of the armistice took place two days later, on December 6, at Austerlitz Castle. This was done in the current historical hall, which had strange acoustics (the architects of the time wanted no one to be able to hear the discussions behind the door). The signing of the document itself was done without the Sovereigns representing the contracting states. It was therefore Prince Johann I of Liechtenstein who signed for the Austrians and Louis-Alexandre Berthier for the French. The clauses of the armistice also ordered the defeated Russia to leave Austrian territory and especially Hungary and Moravia within fifteen days. Those who visit the castle will be disappointed not to find the original bed on which Napoleon had slept. In fact, the exposed bed has been

▲ The armistice plaque of 4 December.

reassembled from various parts from the 18th and 19th centuries. Some of these wooden parts come from other equipment - for example, from a pulpit. It has to be said that, although Napoleon slept in a bed appropriate to his position, he did not care much for luxury. For example, he spent several hours of the night before the battle in a hut temporarily built by his hoesmen on Žuráň. It was typical for him to work hard and sleep little; only a few hours during the day. Before a battle he slept mostly on his military bunk and rarely in a comfortable bed.

The Russians will examine that defeat carefully and the Tsar himself will ask for an official report. Kutuzov will take a year to compile his thoughts on the Austerlitz defeat. On March 13, 1806, he blamed the defeat on Miloradovich and Przibishewski, accusing the latter of having entrenched himself in the village of Kobelnitz *"without having taken security measures, so that the enemy was able to surround him and take most of his soldiers prisoner."* In a letter prior to the report, February 2, 1806, addressed to Kutuzov , General Buxhöwden attributes the defeat to General Langeron *"... for allowing the enemy to attack his rear, without having foreseen it ..."* The most interesting aspect of Buxhöwden's report is not so much the indictment of the various generals, albeit non-Russian, but are some observations that reveal the nature of command in Russia. *"In the past it never happened to see men leaving the battlefield because of a blow or light wounds, everyone tried as far as possible to stay with their units [...] I attribute the responsibility for the bad examples, which have been reported to me, to insubordination, which once did not exist; comparing the relations between subordinates and superiors in rank of the time when we were officers, one cannot help noticing a too sensitive difference. At one time, one could strictly observe a deep respect and trust on the part of the subordinates towards their officers [...] Generals and all those who generally had honors were considered by the subordinates as superior beings with very peculiar qualities, almost supernatural if compared to theirs.*

On the contrary, today there is no respect for rank [...] everyone binds with a mutual familiarity that generates indifference and lack of respect for the superior. Some may find blind the ancient subordination of subordinates, but it was the cause of the successes of times past; we must absolutely restore it."

<table><tr><td>

Buxhöwden's apologia is an apologia for the old Frederickian principle that the soldier should fear his officer more than the enemy. Familiarity of relationships is considered a disaster and as the main cause of defeat. This is a total difference from what happened in the Grande Armée, where officer familiarity was often considered an added moral value; where officer charisma and honor were the driving values. For these reasons, the French soldier had the opportunity and was encouraged to move up through the ranks. General Buxhöwden's summation also revealed the profound difference between two societies, one formally made up of people equal before the Law, the other founded on the privileges of the aristocracy.

</td></tr></table>

Austerlitz, according to the Russian military was lost by the Coalition because of the "French" Langeron, condemned by a disgraceful commission of inquiry, chaired by one of the main defendants, Miloradovich. The fact will be the origin of the famous vitriolic memoirs of General Emigré, taken up, like a gospel, by almost all posthumous historians. Russian diplomats, however, blamed the Austrians and their Chief of Staff, Franz von Weyrother; the Austrians, resigned, sketched. Kutuzov vigorously rejected all charges regarding the Battle Plan and approaching the Guard's grenadier regiment, Izmailovski, conversed with an officer, saying, "I wash my hands of it." Seven years later, during the campaign of 1812, after repelling the French, while standing on a bench sheltered from the rain by some captured French flags, he noticed, on one of them the inscription "For the Battle of Austerlitz." Turning to those present he said: *"Gentlemen, you are young and you will outlive me, you will hear about our wars. In addition to everything that has happened today before your eyes, one more success or one more defeat is of no value to my military career and is indifferent to my glory. But remember this! I am not responsible for anything in regard to the defeat at Austerlitz."*

According to Russian sources there was no command unit, each column leader did as he pleased, according to his inspiration. The orders taken by Langeron and Przbishevski were contradictory, so much so that the former was asked to resign. The letter addressed to him by Count Lieven for the occasion, was corrected by hand by the Czar himself. It said thus: "*The events of the day of November 20 (December 2 according to the Russian calendar) were rather unfortunate for the column under Your Excellency's command, Your Majesty was not very satisfied with the manner in which this column was conducted and, by means of this letter and in order to meet your courtesy, grants you the faculty of asking for your resignation.*" Przbishevski was brought before a War Tribunal on the charge of having surrendered at the beginning of the battle. Eventually the Tribunal admitted that he was taken prisoner at the end of the battle. After the sentence reached the Imperial Court (Military Supreme Court) the charges were changed to a) lack of precise instructions to the generals of the column and b) lack of connection with other columns and lack of measures to ensure the retreat into Hungarian territory. Przbishevski was thus discharged and demoted; he had to serve as a private in a regiment for one month. On November 25, 1810, the Tsar confirmed the sentence. Two battalions of the Novgorod regiment were found guilty of serious disorder. The Tsar ordered that all officers and graduates should carry swords without dragons, that soldiers should be deprived of their sabers and that their service should be extended to 5 years. The same punishments were extended to all those who had abandoned their units.

According to the writer, instead, it is more appropriate to think that the decisive phase of the French victory took place in the most dangerous part of the line-up, to the south, that is to the right of Napoleon, where about 30,000 Austro-Russians were arriving and where the defense was fierce.

▲ Napoleon and Francis II after the battle of Austerlitz. Painting by Antoine-Iean Gros.

AUSTERLITZ: THE DEPLOYMENTS

The whole of Europe knows this place by the name it had at the time of the event: Austerlitz, the German name of the town where peace was signed. Now that town is called by its Czech name: Slavkov. On the maps, therefore, if you want to find Austerlitz you have to look for Slavkov u Brna, and this, for those who do not know, is a first difficulty.

Then, for the identification of the area: because Slavkov (or Austerlitz) is the place where, inside the historic palace, was signed the armistice that ended the hostilities (the peace treaty was then signed in Presburg, today Bratislava), while the battle was not fought in Slavkov, but on an area of vast extension, located between Brno and Slavkov, which includes several very small villages, not far from the international airport of Brno. Today the place is quite well signaled, but however to reach it easily you need specific information, some of which can be found here.

> **Slavkov u Brna (Austerlitz)** - Austerlitz is the German name for this village. It has a baroque palace, belonging to the Kounic family, designed by an Italian architect, Domenico Martinelli. The three emperors all stayed there before or after the battle. On December 6, the armistice was signed here in the Hall of Mirrors and Napoleon addressed a proclamation to the crowd from the balcony of the palace. Famous is his phrase: *"If you say - I was there at Austerlitz - everyone will answer - You are a hero!"*

THE BATTLEFIELD

The Battle of Austerlitz involved three major armies, the French, Austrian, and Russian, totaling nearly 160,000 men. About 73,000 were the French, and more than 85,000 were the Austro-Russians. The front of the battle, which took place throughout the day of December 2, 1805, covered a very large area of about 120 km2, in which there were about thirty towns and villages, halfway between **Brno** (Brünn) and **Slavkov** (Austerlitz). The French army, coming from the west, was lined up, with its back to Brno, in front of the Austro-Russian army coming from the south (Austrians) and from the east (Russians). The following tables show the atmospheric variations at the time of the battle and the solar excursion on December 1 and 2, 1805. The weather report of that time gives an account of very cloudy skies, so we do not know if the famous "Austerlitz Sun" really peeped through the clouds or was only a metaphor.

As for the battlefield, we can identify three major areas of confrontation, corresponding, from north to south, to the left wing, the center, and the French right wing.

TEMPO	TEMPERATURA		VENTO		NUVOLOSITA'		METEO
DATA	giorno (media)	notte	direzione	intensità	giorno	notte	
30-nov	2°	0,9	S-SE	debole	COPERTO	id	NEVE
01-dic	2,5°	2°	S-SE	media	COPERTO	id	NEBBIA
02-dic	5,2°	3,6°	SE	debole	MOLTO NUVOLOSO	id	NEBBIA PIOGGIA
03-dic	2,5°	0,9°	NO- N	debole	MOLTO NUVOLOSO	COPERTO	NEVISCHIO

1805	Sunrise/Sunset		Daylength	
dic	Sunrise	Sunset	Length	Difference
▾ 1	7.24 ↘ (123')	15.56 ↗ (236')	8:31:38	−1:55
▾ 2	7.25 ↘ (124')	15.55 ↗ (236')	8:29:49	−1:49

▲ The sun at Brno in this day

THE NORTHERN SECTOR OR FRENCH LEFT WING

The French left wing was composed of **Lannes' V Corps** or Suchet and Caffarelli divisions and was deployed in the vicinity of the village of Bosenitz (today Tvarožná) and the Santon hill.

Bosenitz (Tvarožná) is a village known since 1288. The village has a replica of a French Gribeauval cannon in front of the town hall. Today it is known as the site of the battle reenactment. Nearby is the Santon, a famous fortified hill. It was called Padělek or Tvarožná Hill. Napoleon had ordered Brigadier Michel Claparède to deploy his 17th regiment of light infantry inside three rings of trenches, which circled the hill, reinforced by the fire of 18 pieces, under the command of Gen. Sénarmont. The hill was called Le Santon by the French (apparently because it recalled a similarly shaped hill that had been noted in Egypt - imperial sources, and a painting, said it was the site of a wedding chapel dedicated to St.Anton = Santon). The little church of Our Lady of the Snows or the Holy Virgin had been torn down by the French before the battle to make trenches. It will be rebuilt in 1832 (it had memorial plaques of the French generals Claparède, Valhubert and the Russian general Bagration). On the Santon was wounded and the general - Jean Marie Roger Valhubert, who died a few days later in Brno and was buried in the former cemetery of the city, today Tyrš where there is a memorial.

▲ Santobin hill with the Saint Nicolas chapel.

Tvarožná - Blažovice (Bosenitz - Blasowitz) - The crossroad

The area was the scene of epic cavalry clashes, perhaps the most epic charges in Napoleonic history. South of the road junction, 20,000 cavalrymen clashed in numerous waves between 9 and 11 am. It was here that Napoleon's brother-in-law, Joachim Murat, gained his reputation for leading cavalry armies. The commander of the Austrian cavalry, FML Johamn Joseph zu Liechtenstein, master of the palace in nearby Pozořice, was able to keep up with him.

French wing deployments

NORTH of the road to Olomouc (Olmütz) Suchet and d'Hautpoul were deployed under the command of Lannes.

V Marshall Jean Lannes Corp

3rd Division (général-de-division or GdD) Louis Gabriel Suchet

1st Brigade (général-de-brigade or GdB) Michel Marie Claparède

17th light infantry regiment 2 btg - 1373 - Col. Dominique Honoré Antoine Marie Vedel (in the Santon trenches)

2nd Brigade GdB Nicolas Léonard Bagert Beker

34th regiment of Line 2 btg- 1615 - Colonel Jean Antoine Dejean

40th Line regiment 2 btg - 1149 - Colonel François Marc Guillaume Legendre d'Harvesse

3rd Brigade GdB Jean Marie Mellon Roger Valhubert

64th Line 2 btg - 1052 - Colonel Claude Nerin

88th Line Regiment 2 btg - 1428 - Colonel Philibert Jean Baptiste François Curial

Artillery 15th Company 5th Regiment Foot - 8 pieces / 16th Company 5th Regiment Foot - 2 pieces / 5th Company 1st Regiment Foot - 4 pieces. (191 men).

A regular Battery of foot artillery would have had: 1 12-pounder cannon + 4 8-pounder cannons + 1 4-pounder cannon.

2nd Heavy Cavalry Division GdD Jean Joseph Ange d'Hautpoul

1st Brigade Adjutant-Commandant François Xavier Octavie Fontaine (replaced by Colonel Noirot)

1st Regiment Cuirassiers 3 squadrons (sq.) - 298 - Colonel Marie Adrian François Guiton

5th Regg. Cuirassiers 3 Sq. - 270 - Colonel Jean Baptiste Noirot

2nd Brigade GdB Raymond Gaspard de Bonardi count de Saint Sulpice

10th Regiment Cuirassiers - 3 Sq. - 224 - Colonel Pierre François Lataye

11th Regg. Cuirassiers - 3 Sq. - 251 - Colonel Albert Louis Emmanuel Fouler

Artillery - 4th Company, 2nd Mounted Regiment - 3 pieces (85 men).

A regular half horse battery would have had 2 8-pounder cannons + 1 howitzer and 44 men.

SOUTH of the road to Olomouc-Beaumont, Caffarelli, Kellerman, Nansouty and Walther divisions under Murat's command.

Reserve Cavalry Maréchal Joachim Murat

1st Heavy Cavalry Division GdD Etienne Marie Antoine Champion, Comte de Nansouty

1st Brigade GdB Joseph Piston

1st Regt. Carabinieri - 3 sq. 195 - Colonel Antoine Cristophe Cochais (according to other sources Francesco Borghese, future VII prince of Sulmona replaced the titular colonel)

2nd Regt. Carabinieri - 3 sq. 182 - Colonel Pierre Nicolas Morin

2nd Brigade GdB Armand Lebrun Comte de La Houssaye

2nd Regiment Cuirassiers - 3 Sq. 249 - Colonel Jean Frédéric Yvendorf

9th Regt. Cuirassiers - 3 Sq. 250 - Colonel Jean Pierre Doumerc

3rd Brigade GdB Antoine Louis Decrest, Comte de Saint-Germain

3rd Regiment Cuirassiers - 3 Sq. 279 - Colonel Claude Antoine Preval

12th Regiment Cuirassiers - 3 sq. 232 Colonel Jacques Roland Belfort

Artillery: 4th Company of the 2nd Mounted Regiment - 3 pieces and 92 men.

2nd Dragoon Division GdD Frédéric Henri Walther

1st Brigade GdB Horace François Bastien Sebastiani de la Porta

3rd Regiment Dragoons 3 sq. 177 - Colonel Edme Nicolas Fiteau

6th regiment. Dragoons 3 sq. 150 - Colonel Jacques Lebaron

2nd Brigade GdB Mansuy Dominique Roget, Baron de Bellonguet

10th Regt. Dragoons 3 sq. 207 - Colonel Jacques Marie Cavaignac

11th Regt. Dragoons 3 sq. 196 - Colonel Ferdinand Pierre Agathé Bourdon

3rd Brigade GdB André Joseph Boussart

13° Regg. Dragoons 3 sq. 269 - Colonel Armand Louis Broc

22nd Regiment Dragoons 3 sq. 134 - Colonel Jean Auguste Carrié

Artillery: 2nd Company of the 2nd Mounted Regiment - 3 pieces (2 8-pounders + 1 6-inch howitzer) and 84 men.

3rd Dragoon Division GdB Charles Joseph Boyé (for GdD Beaumont, ill, Boyé in command Dec. 2).

1st Brigade GdB Charles Joseph Boyé

5th Regiment Dragoons 3 sq. 234 - Colonel Jacques Nicolas Lacour

8th Regt. Dragoons 3 sq. 289 - Colonel Louis Beckler

12th Regt. Dragoons 3 sq 297 - Colonel Joseph Pagès

2nd Brigade GdB Nicolas Joseph Scalfort

9° Regg. Dragoons 3 sq. 291 - Colonel Pierre Honoré Anne Maupetit

16° Regiment. Dragoons 3 sq. 242 - Colonel François Marie Clément de la Ronciere

21th Regiment Dragoons 3 sq. 285 - Colonel Jean Baptiste Charles Rene Joseph Mas de Polart

Artillery: 3rd Company of the 2nd regiment on horseback - 3 pieces and 85 men.

Light Cavalry Division GdD François Etienne Kellermann (detached from I Corps)

1st Brigade GdB Joseph Denis Picard

2nd regt. Ussari 3 sq. 328 - Colonel Ignace Wilhelm Rith

5th regt. Ussari 3 sq. 342 - Colonel François Xavier Nicolas Schwartz

2nd Brigade GdB Frederic Christophe Henri Pierre Claude Marisy

4th regt Ussari 3 sq. 280 - Colonel André Burthe

5th regt. Chasseurs à cheval 3 sq. 317 - Colonel Claude Louis Constant Esprit Juvenal Corbineau

Light cavalry brigade GdB Edouard Jean Baptiste Milhaud

16th regt. Chasseurs à cheval 3 sq. 205 - Colonel Antoine Jean Auguste Henri Durosnel

22nd regt. Chasseurs à cheval 3 sq. 218 - Colonel Marie Victor Nicolas de Fay, Marquis de Latour-Maubourg

Light cavalry brigade GdB Anne François Charles Trelliard detached from the 5th Corps

9th regt. Ussari 3 sq. 145 - Colonel Etienne Guyot

10th regt. Ussari 3 sq. 161 - Colonel Louis Chrétien Carrière Beaumont

1st Division GdD Louis Marie Joseph Maximilien de Caffarelli du Falga (detached to III Corps ex Lannes)

1st Brigade GdB Joseph Laurent Demont

17th Line 2 btg 1561 - Colonel Nicolas François Conroux

30th Line 2 btg 1011 - Colonel François Valterre

2nd Brigade GdB Jean Louis Debilly

51st Line 2 btg 1214 Colonel Joseph Alphonse Hyacinthe Alexandre Bonnet d'Honnières

61st Line 2 btg 1175 - Colonel Jean Nicolas

3rd Brigade GdB Georges Henri Eppler

13th Light Regiment 2 btg 1240 - Colonel Pierre Castex

Artillery: 1st Company 7th Foot Regiment - 6 pieces (4 8-pounders + 2 6-inch howitzers) 169 men.

▲ French troops array themselves at Austerlitz (reenactors in French uniforms). Courtesy by Keith Redfern.

Represents the initial French position on the northern flank. Marshal Lannes commands the French wing north of the road to Brno; Marshal Murat commands the French cavalry south of the road. He will be confronted by the FML and Duke, Johann Joseph zu Liechtenstein, owner of a nearby castle in Pozořice. The "Rohlenka" inn stood where today there is a restaurant service area on the highway. A mass grave dated 1805 was uncovered during the construction of a McDonald's restaurant (September 1995). Several dozen skeletons testified that there had been a hospital there. From Rohlenka you can see the heights of Žuráň, Santon and Pratzen (Pratecký). On the second floor there is a model of the battle that was opened on July 1, 2002.

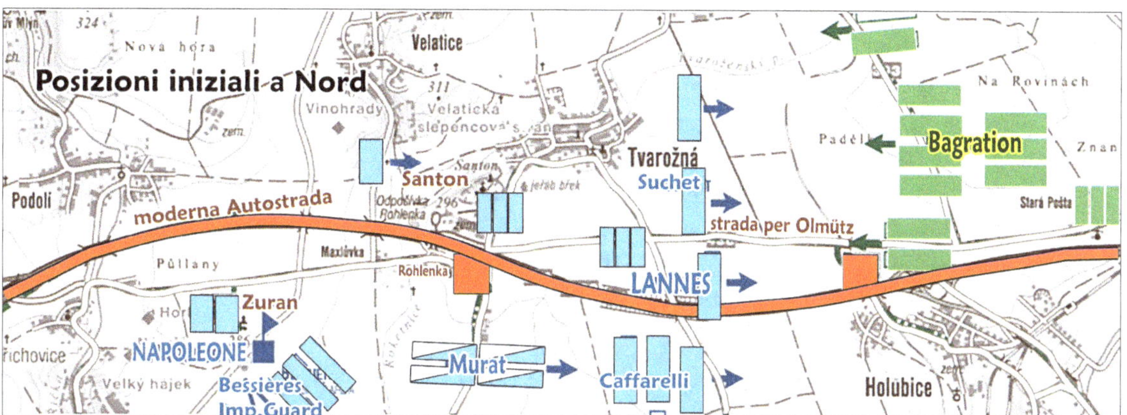

ALLIED DEPLOYMENTS

NORTH of the road to Olomouc - the Russians of Bagration.

Vanguard (General Leutnant or GL) Piotr Ivanovich Bagration

Left flank

- 6 Regt. Eger (Jäger) 3 btg. 364 - Shef GM Karl Karlovich Ulanius - Com Col. (pulkovnik or PK) Ivan Petrovich Beloko-pytov

- Hussars of Mariupol 10 sq. 1234 - Shef GM Piotr Kristianovich Count Witgenshtein or "Wittgenstein" - Com. PK Aleksei Andrejevich Laskin (Shef or Chef = owner of the regiment; GM = generalmaior or major general)

- Don Cossacks Kiseljev 5 sq. 500

- Don Cossacks Malakhov 5 sq. 500

Right flank

- 5th Regt. Eger 2 btg 794 - Shef PK Fiodor Grigorjevich Gogel - com. Maior Fedor lvanovich Pantenius (the III btg. was detached on 29 November to the vanguard of the I Column

- Hussars of Pavlograd 10 sq. 1409 - Shef GL Karl Fiodorovich Bour Sr. (remained in Russia because sick - Sr. com. GM Yefim lgnatievich Chaplits - com. PK Simion Davidovich Panchulidzev

- Don Cossacks Khaznekov 5 sq. 500

- Don Cossacks Sisoiev 5 sq. 500 (maybe they were with Kienmayer)

Brigade GM (Adjutant General) Prince Piotr Piotrovich Dolgoruky

- 3 Regiment Musketeers Staro Ingermanland 3 btg 2023 - Shef GM Grigorii Grigorievich Engelgardt-1 (Engelhardt) Com. ?

- Regt. Musketeers of Pskov 3 btg 2050 - Shef Mikail Ilarionovich Golenishev-Kutuzov - com. GM Evgienii Ivanovich Markov-1

- Regt. Musketeers Arkangelgorod 3 btg 1931 - Shef GM Nikolai Mikhailovich Kamensky-2 - com. PK Mikail Ivanovich Berlizeev

Artillery support 18 pieces

SOUTH of the road to Olomouc - the Austrians of Liechtenstein.
5th Column FML Prince Johann Liechtenstein
Austrian Cavalry Division Lieutenant Field Marshal (FML) Prince Hohenlohe
1st Cavalry Brigade GM Caramelli
- 5th Nassau Regiment of Cuirassiers 6 sq 300 - Oberst (Col.) Friedrich von Minutillo
- 7th Lorraine (Lothringen) Cuirassier Regiment 6 sq 300 - Oberst Clemens Freiherr von Thunefeld
2nd Cavalry Brigade Major General Weber
- 1st Regiment Kaiser Franz 6 sq. - 425h - Oberst Wilhelm von Motzen
Artillery support horse battery 8 pieces 200 men - Captain Zocchi
Russian cavalry division GL Aleksei Aleksevich von Essen-2 (Hessen)
Brigade GM Vasily Fedorovich Shepelev
- Cuirassiers Leib-Kirasirskii E. E. Velichestva 5 sq. 761 - "Cuirassiers of the Tsarina" Shef GM Dmitri Maksimovich Esipov-1 - com. PK Yakovlev Osipovich Count Witi
- Regt. Dragoons of St. Petersburg 2 sq. 200 (sq. IV and V were detached to II Column from 2 December) Shef GL Vasily Fiodorovich Shepelev - com. ?
- Regt. Ulani of Grand Duke Constantine 10 sq 1386 - Shef Grand Duke Konstantin Pavlovich Commandant of the Column of the Guard - com. GM Egor Ianovich Baron Muller-Zakomelsky
- Don Cossacks Gordejev 5 sq. 500
- Don Cossacks Isaiev 4 sq. 500 - (1 sq. detached on December 2 to II Column)
Artillery support: Light battery with 11 pieces (6 cannons of 6 lib. + 5 unicorns of 10 lib.) and 230 men - PK Gabriel Alexandrovich Ignatiev
Brigade GM (adjutant general) Fiodor Piotrovich Uvarov
- Regt. Dragoons of Chernigov 5 sq 782 - Shef GL von Essen-I* (commander of the division) - com. PK Ivan Davidovich Panchulidzev-1
- Regg. Dragoons of Kharkov 5 sq 741 - Shef GM Vartolomei Kaetanovich Gizhitzkii - com. PK Minitzkii
- Regg. Hussars Elisavetgrad 10 sq 1356 - Shef GM Erofei Kus'mich baron von der Osten-Saken-3 - com. PK Grigori Iva-novich Lisanevich
- Don Cossacks Denisov 3 sq. 300
- Don Cossacks Melentjev 5 sq. 500 - (perhaps they were with Kienmayer)
Support artillery: light battery of the 1st btg. st Horse Artillery (12 pieces 230 men) PK Aleksei Piotrovich Jermolov

Holubice (Holubitz). Violent fighting took place between Holubice and Kruh. At 8 a.m. 1000 horsemen of the Bagration column attacked French light cavalry attempting to disengage. The first row of charging Ulans was mowed down by a volley. More than 300 horses died and the rest stumbled over the dead, knocking the horsemen off their feet. The French light cavalry regrouped behind the wall of infantry and set off on a counterattack. The Russian attack became a retreat. Many galloping horses ended up buffeting each other in a slowdown between Kruh and Holubitz. Liechtenstein's resistance, with cavalry, consolidated Bagration's line, stabilizing the Holubitz-Kruh-Posoritz route. The French attack restarted at 11 o'clock commanded by Murat and Lannes, supported by Rivaud's 1st Infantry Division of Bernadotte's 1st Corps. The pressure on Bagration's weak left flank forced the Russians to retreat, which Bagration led in stages on the imperial road to Russínov. The retreat was protected by two Austrian batteries under Major Frierenberger, deployed on high ground between the Old Post (Stará Pošta) and Kovalovitz. Major Frierenberger was awarded the Knight's Cross of Maria Theresa for that action and since 1995 a small memorial commemorating that event has been located at the side of the road to Russínov, at the Kovalovitz-Veleschowitz intersection.

Old mill (Stará Valcha). Part of the Russian regiments of Essen II and Uvarov, under the command of FML Liechtenstein, advanced from Krenovitz along the Rakovec stream towards Holubitz. Here, at Stara Valcha (mill), in the middle of the mota, they joined the Russian Guard, which was coming down from Austerlitz, via Krenovitz. The commander of the Guard, Grand Duke Con-Stantin Pavlovich, deployed the troops in two lines (infantry in front and cavalry behind). The Russian line succeeded in blocking Caffarelli's advance from Holubitz.

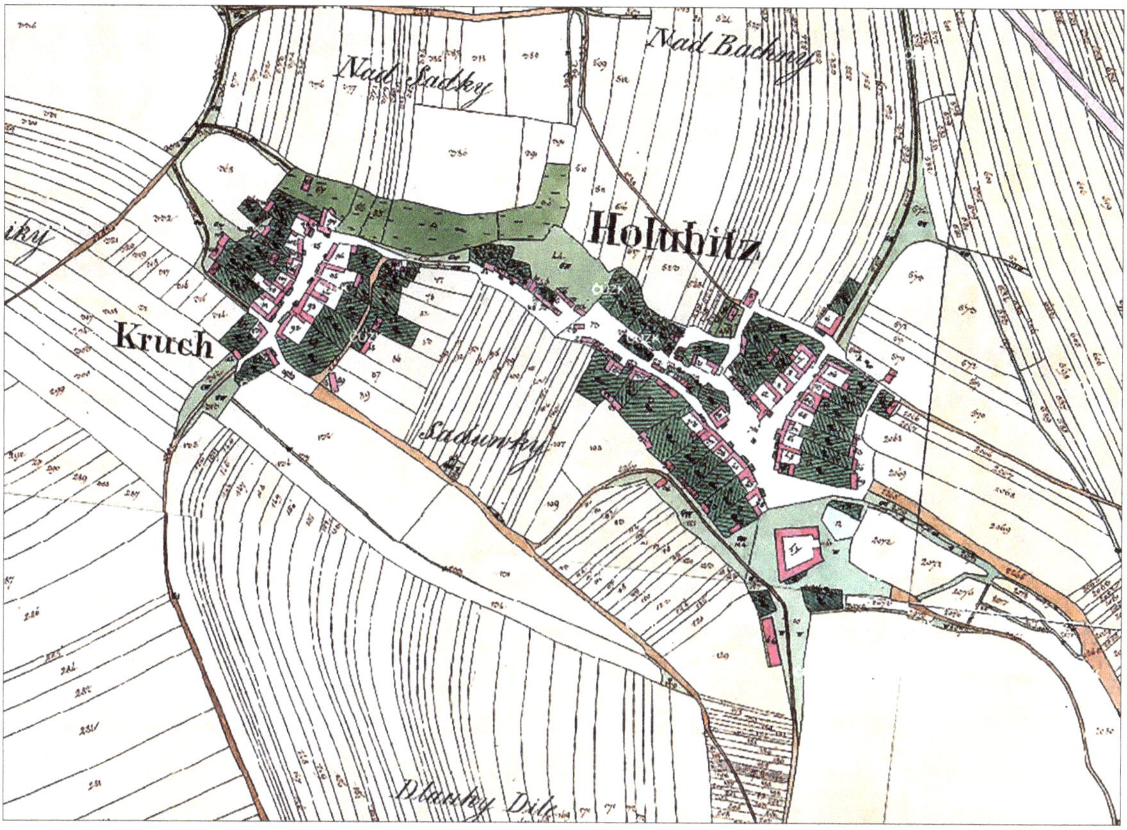

Stará Pošta (the old Post Office) Important cities were once connected by postal routes on which there were stations located at an interval of two Viennese miles, about fifteen kilometers. Thanks to the change of horses, couriers could keep to the prescribed speed for the route. One of the post stations was located, since 1785, on the imperial road between Brno and Olomouc not far from Pozořice and Kovalovice. The old Posoritz Post Office is still located halfway between Brno and Vyškov and has been preserved. The HQs of both adversaries, for some and different periods of time, were in this building. In November 28, Napoleon was there with Berthier, Soult and Lannes (it was Murat's HQ). The Russians advancing from Olomouc, with Bagration, occupied the Post Office before the battle. Liechtenstein, among other things master of the Post Office as master of Pozoritz, met the envoy of the Emperor of Austria nearby after the battle. They agreed to negotiate a truce at the Burnt Stream Mill (today Spálený mlýn). From the Old Post Office, Napoleon then took himself to the Austerlitz Palace (Slavkov Castle) to sign the armistice. Near the Post Office is the memorial that recalls the Frierenberger affair recounted above.

Pozořice (Posoritz) The French occupied Posoritz, the village owned by the Liechtensteins, who had a palace, court, distillery, brewery and market there, on 19 November. Milhaud and 15 soldiers spent the night in the rectory of the Chapel of St. Nicholas. After Milhaud, the Adjutant General Fontaine and his staff stayed there until November 29, 1805. After the battle, the village was sacked. It seems that an alleged mass grave is located near the old brick factories and the "Dvoje" (two lines).

Lichy
Zahradky
IV
Brnensky Pole
Ssirohy Pole
Markt Schlapanitz
Zahumenize

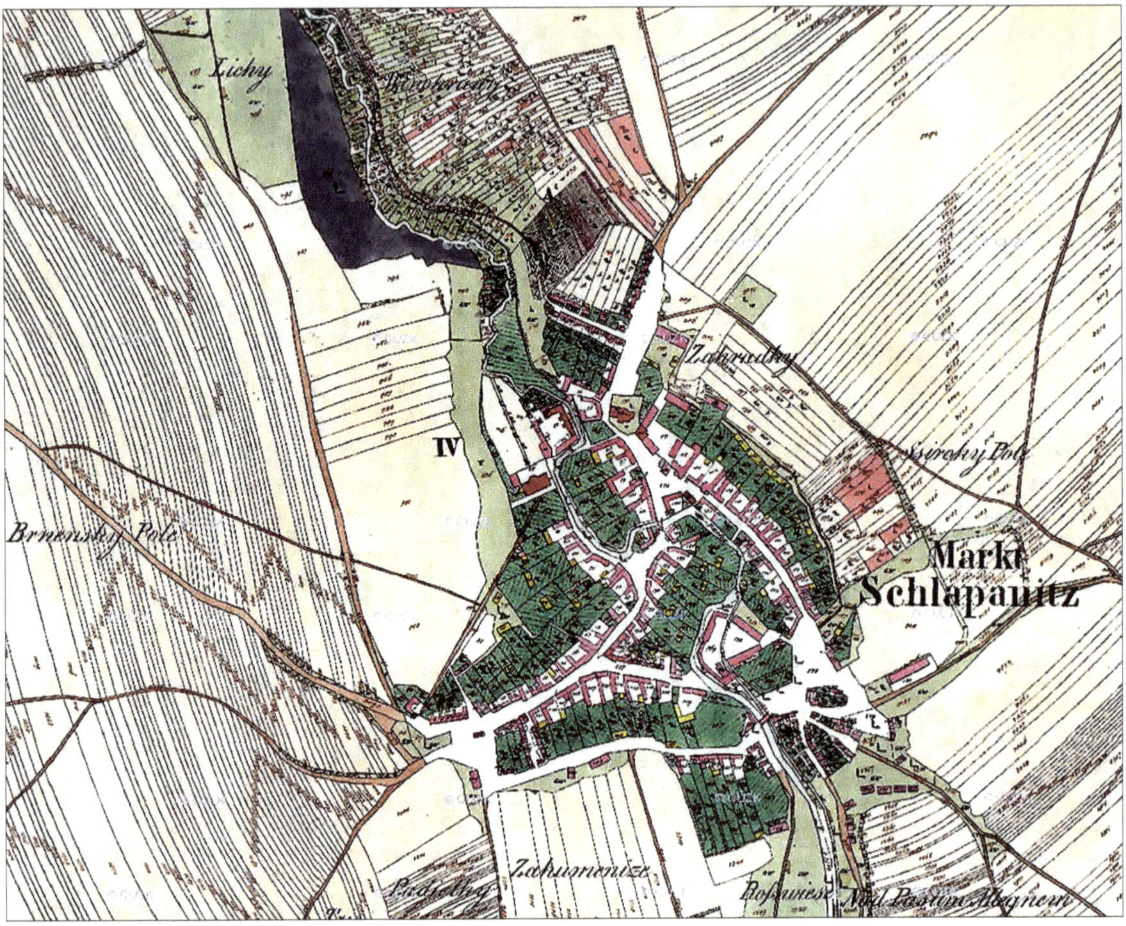

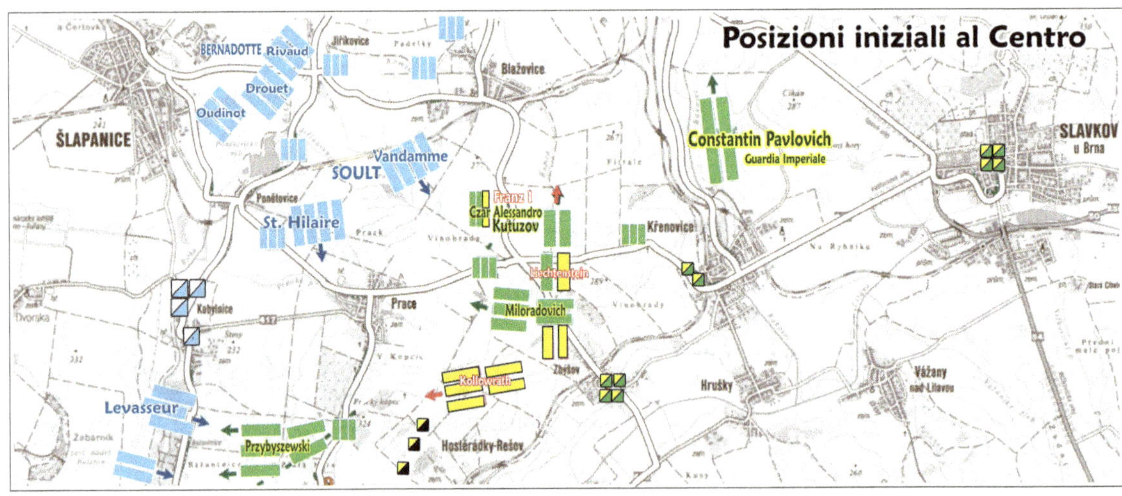

Posizioni iniziali al Centro
BERNADOTTE Rivaud
Drouet
Oudinot
ŠLAPANICE
Jiříkovice
Blažovice
SOULT
Vandamme
Ponětovice
St. Hilaire
Franz I
Czar Alessandro
Kutuzov
Liechtenstein
Miloradovich
Kollowrath
Constantin Pavlovich
Guardia Imperiale
SLAVKOV
u Brna
Křenovice
Kobylnice
Prace
Zbýšov
Hrušky
Vážany
nad Litavou
Levasseur
Przybyszewski
Hostěrádky-Rešov

THE CENTRAL SECTOR

The center of the French army was deployed in the valley of the Žuráň hill, about a kilometer from the village of Schlapanitz. In front of the Zuran was Bessières with the Guard.

Commander in Chief Emperor Napoleon I
General Staff : Emperor's aides-de-camp : GdD Junot and Savary - GdB Rapp, Bertrand, Gardanne, Lemarois, and Mouton - Col. Lebrun, Caffarelli, Lauriston, Reille. **Emperor's ordnance officers :** Castille, Eugène de Monte-squiou, Amédée de Turenne, Falkouwski, Deponthon, Scher, Bongard, Berthemy, Maulnois, Parrain
Army Chief of Staff : Maréchal Louis-Alexandre Berthier with Captains Colbert, Girardin, Lejeune and Lieutenants Perigord and Lagrange. **Chief of General Staff:** DD Andreossy; **Maréchal des logis :** DD Dumas ; **Artillery Commander:** DD Songis; **Chief of Staff of Artillery:** DD Pernetti; **Deputy Chief of Staff of Artillery:** Col Senarmont; **Commandant of the Engineer Corps:** DD Marescot; **Chief of Staff of the Engineer Corps:** Maj-Gen Ducoudsary: **Director of the Telegraph:** Chappe; **Chief of Bakery:** Le Payen ; **Chief Surgeon:** Poussielgue; **Grand Marshal of the Palace:** GdD Duroc; **Grand Squire:** GdD Caulaincourt; **Military Administrator:** Pierre A. Daru.
Grand Army Artillery Park (230 men) one foot battery (6 pieces with 3-pound Austrian guns and an unknown number of howitzers); two foot batteries (6 pieces with 12-pound guns and an unknown number of howitzers) all operated by the 7th Artillery Regiment.
Imperial Guard of Emperor Napoleon I Maréchal Jean Baptiste Bessières
1st Brigade GdB Pierre Auguste Hulin (actually Hulin was absent because he commanded in Vienna)
Grenadiers à Pied 2 btg. 1519 - Colonel-Major Jean Marie Pierre François Lepaige Dorsenne
2nd Brigade GdB Jerome Soulès
Chasseurs à Pied 2 btg - 1613 - Major Jean Louis Gros
3rd Brigade GdB Teodoro Lechi Italian Guard
Grenadiers à Pied 1 btg. and Chasseurs à Pied in all 753 men.
French Imperial Guard Cavalry or Gendarmerie d'Elite seconded to Brno
1st Brigade GdB Michel Ordener
Grenadiers à Cheval 4 sq. - 706 - Colonel-Major Louis Lepic
2nd Brigade Colonel-en-Second François Louis de Morland
Chasseurs à Cheval 4 sq, 375 - Colonel-en-Second Nicolas Dahlmann
Mamluks half sq. - 48 - Chef d'Escadron Antoine Charles Bernard Delaitre
Artillery of the Guard (col. Couin) (540 u.) : 1st Comp. on horseback 8 pieces (4 cannons of 8 lib. - 2 canons of 4 lib. - 2 howitzers of 6 inches) - 2nd Comp. on horseback 8 pieces (4 cannons of 8 lib. - 2 canons of 4 lib. - 2 howitzers of 6 inches) - Mounted Artillery of the Italian Royal Guard 8 pieces (4 cannons of 8 lib. - 2 canons of 4 lib. - 2 howitzers of 6 inches)
Marine Infantry or Bataillon de Marins 1btg. 120 - Com. François-Henri-Eugene Daugier.

► Pindulka tavern

Žuráň **Hill (pronounced Jouránii, not Zurlan)** On Žuráň Hill Napoleon set up his headquarters and directed operations from there. Today there is a marble plinth with a bronze panel above it, illustrating the deployment of the armies. The small piece of land in the Žuráň region on which the base with the battle map stands is, according to an international agreement, an extraterritorial area of France. The significant hill is part of the village of Podolí (then Kritschen), about 1 km north of Šlapanice, and may have been an artificial hillock, with graves dating back to the period of migration of peoples from the 5th-6th centuries. From here, there is a view of the predominant part of the Austerlitz battlefield. From Šlapanice to Žurán, the easiest access is a leisurely walk of about 25 minutes.

It is also notable as an important archaeological site. Probably the first archaeological discoveries on Žuráň date back to 1850. On the large upper surface of the spur of the hill, a remarkable building made of stone, or rather, with a perimeter wall of dry-laid stones, about 80 meters in diameter, was discovered. It seems that the building was even larger since, for centuries, it served the inhabitants of the surrounding communities as a reserve of building stone. It is a circular necropolis in which graves of different historical periods were found, all looted before 1800.

Details of the route

1---Emperor Napoleon and his staff dined at Pindulka, a nearby inn, the night before the battle. He ordered his favorite meal - onion potatoes. The name of the inn came from the name of the former owner, the Brno bourgeois Matěj Pindula. Today the building is used by the Moravian Road Administration and is therefore not open to the public. A few nights before the battle, Napoleon had slept in a nearby place, the Kandia inn near the old road to Olomouc. He wanted to know the terrain he would choose for the future battlefield.

2--- Later, Napoleon rested for a short time, in a makeshift hut, not far from a quarry. During the night, he received a message regarding the strategic plans of the Allied armies for the upcoming battle. They intended to turn the French army from the south, cut off the escape route to Vienna, from where reinforcements were expected to arrive, and drive it back towards the Bohemian-Moravian Alps.

3---The block-post maneuver, to the north, was to be made by Bagration's column, but Napoleon responded with a daring countermove in the direction of the Pratecký (Pratzen) Hills. The maneuver, later dubbed "Lion's Leap," was to be preceded by the gathering of a strong battle group, in the little valley of the Rokytnice stream, between the Žuráň and the Pratecký hills, before dawn.

4--- Shortly before 8 a.m., (Monday, December 2), they say with the sun already high on the horizon of the Pratzen heights, after a quick consultation on the Žuráň, Napoleon ordered Soult, to launch the decisive attack.

5--- the attack started in the direction of the Old Vineyards (Staré Vinohrady) and the Pratecký or Pratzen heights.

In Schlapanitz was deployed the:

1st Elite Division (Grenadiers) GdD Nicolas Charles Oudinot

GdD Géraud Christophe Michel Duroc - detached from the 5th Corps shared the command.

1st Brigade GdB Claude Joseph de Laplanche-Morthières

1st Elite Regiment - 2 btg- 762 - companies from the 13th and 58th Line - Colonel Jacques Froment

2nd Elite Regiment - 2 btg - 1025 - companies from the 9th and 81st Line - Major Michel Sylvestre Brayer

2nd Brigade GdB Pierre Louis Dupas

3rd Elite Regiment - 2 btg - 941 - companies from the 2nd and 3rd light - Colonel Jean Adam Schramm

4th elite regiment 2 btg - 857- companies from 28th and 31st light - Major Marc Cabannes de Puymisson

3rd Brigade GdB François Amable Ruffin

5th elite regiment 2 btg - 1070 - companies from the 12th and 15th light - Colonel Jean Charles Desailly

Artillery (339 u.) - 1st Comp. of 1st Regiment on foot 6 pieces (4 8-pounder + 2 4-pounder cannons) - 4th Comp. of 5th Regiment on horseback 2 pieces (2 8-pounder cannons).

Šlapanice (Lapanz/Schlapanitz) in 1805 had 900 inhabitants and made bread and milk for the city of Brno. On his way from Vienna to Olomouc, the Russian FM Kutuzov had stopped there with his Stavka on the evening of November 17. The Austrian FML Liechtenstein stayed, instead, in the parish on November 19 with the troops camped in the meadows. The French occupied it on November 20. Soult stayed in the building of the present museum, commanding the vanguard. Nansouty, who commanded the cavalry of the Murat column and the entire Reserve (Oudinot's Grenadiers with 40 cannons) were northwest of Šlapanice. After the battle, 400 Russian prisoners were herded into the Church. Hundreds of wounded were treated in a field hospital by a surgical team stationed at the Blümegen Palace. The GdB Thiébault and Valhubert, who later died in Brno, were first treated here. The village and the neighboring districts suffered extensive damage. On the facade of a house at 6 Jiříkovská Street there is a column with a memorial cross and at the cemetery there is a stele commemorating the Šlapanice victims of 1805.

IV Marshal Nicolas Jean-de-Dieu Soult Corps
Artillery reserve: detachments of the 17th and 18th companies of the 5th Foot Regiment (6 12-pounders)
1st Division GdD Louis Vincent Joseph Saint-Hilaire
1st Brigade GdB Charles Antoine Louis Alexis Morand
10th Light Regiment 2 btg 1488 - Col. Pierre Charles Pouzet
2nd Brigade GdB Paul Charles François Adrien Henri Dieudonné, Baron Thiébault
14th Line 2 btg 2051 - Col. Jacques François Marc Mazas
36th Line Regiment 2 btg 1592 Col. Antoine Charles Houdard de Lamotte
3rd Brigade GdB Louis Prix Varé
43rd Line 2 btg 1593 Col. Guillaume Raymond Amant Viviès
55th Line Regiment 2 btg 1614 Col. François Roch Ledru des Essarts
Artillery (120 u.) 12th comp. and detachment of 16th comp. of 5th Regiment on foot - 8 pieces (2 8-pounders + 2 4-pounders + 2 6-inch howitzers) (2 8-pounders) - 230 u. including train.
2nd Division GdD Dominique Joseph René Vandamme
1st Brigade GdB Joseph François Ignace Maximilien Schiner
24th Light Regiment 2 btg 1310 - Col. Bernard Pourailly
2nd Brigade GdB Claude François Ferey
46th Line Regiment 2 btg 1559 - Col. Guillaume Latrille de Lorencez
57th Line Regiment 2 btg 1771 - Col. Jean Pierre Antoine Rey
3rd Brigade GdB Jacques Lazare de Savetier de Candras
4th Line 2 btg 1822 - Maj. Auguste Julien Bigarré
28th Line Regiment 2 btg 1636 - Col. Jean Georges Edighoffen
Artillery: (117 u.) 13th comp. of the 5th Regiment on foot - 6 pieces (2 cann. of 8 lbs. + 2 cann. of 4 lbs. + 2 howitzers of 6 inches) - di-station of the 16th comp. of the 5th Regiment on foot (2 cann. of 8 lbs.)

I Corp Marshal Jean Baptiste Jules Bernadotte
1st Division GdD Olivier Macoux Rivaud de la Raffinière
1st Brigade GdB Charles Dumoulin
8th Line Regiment 3 btg 1858 - Col. Jean François Etienne Autie
45th Line Regiment 3 btg 1603 - Col. Jean Leonard Barrie.
2nd Brigade GdB Michel Marie Pacthod
54th line regiment 3 btg 1614 - Col. Armand Philippon
Artillery: (191 u.) 1st comp. of the 8th on foot 6 pieces (4 cann. of 3 lbs. and a howitzer of 5 1/3 inches) - 2nd comp. of the 3rd regiment on horseback 6 pieces (4 cann. of 3 lbs. and a howitzer of 5 1/3 inches)
2nd Division GdD Jean Baptiste Drouet (Count of Erlon since 1806)
1st Brigade GdB François Jean Werle
27th Light Regiment 3 btg 2069 - Col. Jean Baptiste Charnotet
2nd Brigade GdB Bernard Georges François Frère
94th Line Regiment 3 btg 1814 - Col. Jean Nicolas Razout
95th line regiment 3 btg 1903 - Col. Marc Nicolas Louis Pechaux
Artillery (229 u.) : 2nd comp. of the 8th regiment on foot 6 pieces (5 cann. of 3 lbs. and a howitzer of 5 1/3 inches) - 3rd comp. of the 3rd regiment on horseback 6 pieces (4 cann. of 3 lbs. and a howitzer of 5 1/3 inches).

Jiříkovice (Girzikowitz) in 1805 had three masters; the Braid counts of the Šlapanice Lower Court, the Dietriechstein falconry estate, and the St. Anne's Convent in Brno. Jiříkovice is located southeast of Žuráň, limited to the north by the Olomouc road. The

Legend says that the founder was a certain Jiří (George) who gave his name to the village. They say that in Girzikowitz, where Soult's corps was deployed, on the eve of the battle, Napoleon inspected the position of his units. Impromptly, he stumbled in the dark, perhaps he in a stump or a sleeping soldier. The soldier lit a wisp of straw to light the way for the emperor. Soon others joined in, shouting *"Vive l'Empreur!"* and raising flaming straw with their weapons. The singularity of this moment was indescribable. But the straw burned quickly and the fire demanded more food. They began to use stubble from the roofs of the houses and barns in Jiříkovice. Moreover, since the soldiers, who were camped in the surroundings of the village, had already used everything they could burn for heating, windows of the houses and cut trees fell victim to the fires. The event went down in history as the **"Fires of Jiříkovice"**.

There was a French field hospital on a farm near the estate. Some notebooks of a French medical officer were handed down (December 10) which noted the burial of, among others, Colonel Lacon, Major Kuna and Captain Heudelin of the 16th Dragoons. The hospital admitted more than 8 officers and 62 soldiers of both armies. The mass grave is located at the crossroads of the road to Tvarožná, where there is also a memorial erected in 2000.

To the south of the two villages of Blasowitz and Girzikowitz, the infantry of Saint Hilaire and Vandamme, under the command of Soult and Bernadotte, concentrated the night before the battle. The troops, concealed by a thick fog, began the ascent to the heights of Pratzen towards the Old Vineyards (Staré Vinohrady), around 8:30. They crossed the village of Prace (Pratzen) almost razed to the ground by cannon fire (hundreds of soldiers lost their lives there). After a 4-hour battle, Napoleon decided to cut the enemy device in two. They say that the Romza stream between Blažovice and Jiříkovice was red with blood.

THE COALITION CENTER

It necessarily had a defensive character, since the plan of attack demanded a conversion to the south.

IV Miloradovich and Kollowrath column

Vanguard GM Wodniansky

- 1st Regt. Austrian Dragoons Archduke (Erzherzog) Johann 2 sq. 125 - Oberst Ludwig Ritter von Hentzy

- Regt. Russian Musketeers of Novgorod 2 btg, 825 (II-III btg) com. PPK Fiodor Fiodorovich Monakhtin

- Regiment Apsheron Musketeers 1 btg, 402 - Capt. Morozov

- Austrian Pioneer Company Dreier, 160

Russian Division GL Mikail Andrejevich Miloradovich

Miloradovich had been promoted to General Leutnant (lieutenant general on November 8, 1805)

Brigade GM Sergei Yakovich Repninsky

- Regt. Musketeers of Novgorod 1 btg. 412 - Shef GM Sergei Yakovlevich Repninsky, the brigade commander, com. lieutenant colonel (or PPK) Fiodor Fiodorovich Monakhtin, were the vanguard of the IV Column

- Regt. Musketeers of Apsheron 2 btg 805 (II and III) - Shef GM Mikail Andrejevich Miloradovich * division commander - com. PPK Aleksei Vasilievich Prince Sibirsky-l

Brigade GM Grigorii Maksimovich Berg

- Regg. Grenadiers Lesser Russia (Malorossiisky) 3 btg 1446 - Shef "ad honorem" Karl ludwig Friedrich von Baden - com. GM Grigorii Maksimovich Berg, commander of the brigade

- Regt. Musketeers of Smolensk 3 btg 1398 - Shef GM Piotr Mikailovich Koliubakin - com. PK Leontii Kristoforovich baron von der Osten Sacken.

Artillery had 24 "battalion" guns (3- and 6-pounder pieces or 10-pound Unicorns) and the 3rd regiment's position battery with 12 pieces (250 u.) - PK Dmitri Ivanovich Kudriatsev.

Austrian Division Feldzeugmeister (FZM) Johann Karl Count Kollowrath-Krakowsky

Brigade Oberst (Colonel) Ferdinand Baron (Freiherr) von Sterndahl (provisional brigadier)

- Regiment of Line IR 23 Salzburg 6 btg - 2800 - part of the Rottermund Marching Brigade - Col. Ferdinand von Sterndahl

Marching Brigade GM Count Rottermund

- One btg, Line Regiment IR 20 Kaunitz 300 (VI march brigade) - Maj. von Breslern

- One btg. of IR 24 Auersperg 600 (VI march btg.) - Oberstleutnant Bach von Ulm

- One btg. of Line Regt. IR 1 Kaiser Franz, 700 (VI btg. part of the Jurczik marching brigade) - com. ?

- A btg. of IR 9 Czartoryski Line Regiment, 600 (II btg. part of the Jurczik Marching Brigade) - Hauptmann Graf Orlandini (was the garrison of Ofen - today's Budapest)

Marching Brigade GM von Jurczik

- One btg. of the IR 55 Reuss-Greitz Line Regiment, 300 (VI btg.) Oberstleutnant Scovaud

- One bt. of Regiment IR 38 Württemberg, 500 (III btg) Maj-Gen Lornpret

- A btg. of Line Regiment IR 58 Beaulieu, 500 (III btg), com. ??

- One btg. of IR 49 Kerpen Line Regiment, 312 (VI btg) Maj.

- One btg. of IR 29 Lindenau Line Regiment, 400 (VI btg.) com. ??

Support artillery 8 position pieces - 200 u. and 28 battalion guns.

Cavalry detachment Oberstleutnant Rakovsky coming from Kienmayer's advance guard with 2 squadrons of the 4th Regiment. Hussars Hessen-Homburg and one Grenzer squadron of the 11th regiment. Székler Hussars.

Staré Vinohrady (Old Vineyard) (between Blažovice and Zbýšov). A hill (296 meters high) that was at the center of the battle. It was Kutuzov's headquarters. From 8 a.m. on December 2, 1805, there, Emperors Franz I and the Czar, Alexander, would follow the movements of the French, watching the descent of their troops towards Sokolnitz, as per the plan of General Franz von Weyrother. On the hill remain only the divisions of General Miloradovich and Kollo-wrat to hold the impact of the assault of Soult and Bernadotte. In the battle of 4 hours will also intervene the Russian Guard, under the command of the Tsar's brother, Constantin Pavlovich. Before 12 o'clock the French will be in superiority, forcing the Tsar to leave the battlefield. Napoleon descended from Žuráň and crossed the Old Vineyards (Staré vinohrady) to climb the hills of Pratzen, up to the chapel of St. Anton, above Újezd, from where he will observe the retreat of the Allies, through the ponds of Satschan and Menin, beaten by French artillery.

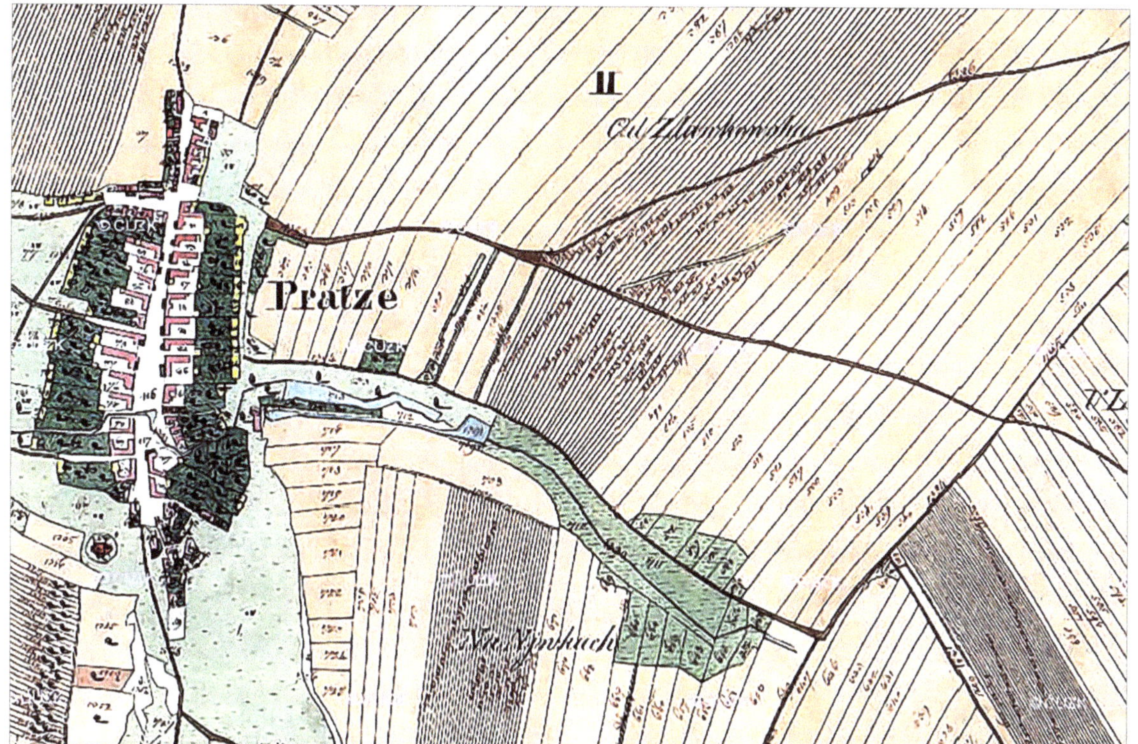

Note on the Austrian infantry: the old organization of 1802, with the Mack reform, provided for different staffs in case of war. In July 1805, for example, the 9th Czartoryski Regiment changed its formation, starting from the usual 20 Companies (3 battalions of 6 companies and a division, or two companies, of Grenadiers) to 5 agile battalions of 4 Companies, 1 Grenadier battalion and 4 battalions of riflemen. The deposit of the recruits formed the VI battalion (sometimes called of March because in practice it was sent to the front to provide replacements for the regular battalions. First it was decided that, in addition to the original grenadier companies, the best rifle divisions would be reported by the command, one of which would be deployed in the middle, between the 2 actual grenadier companies, with, in endowment, not the grenadier headgear, but the normal helmet. They were renamed as "Jung Grenadiers". Naturally, this reorganization made obsolete the old battalion designations of Leib-, Obrist- and Obristlieutenants-Bataillon, as well as the similar designation of the staff companies (Stabs-Compagnien) with the name of the Owner (Inhaber); the rifle battalions took the numbers 1., 2., 3. and 4.; Divisions and Companies continued to bear the name of the commander. Battalion auxiliaries (Bataillons-Adjutanten) were also created. The pomades and powders for the soldiers' hair were eliminated, ordering that the hair should not exceed the length of half a Zoll (1 and a half cm).

High Command of the Coalition Infantry Gen. Mikail Ilarionovich Kutuzov

Tsar Alexander I and the emperor of SRI - Franz I

The Tsar was the de facto commander-in-chief, while Kutuzov was the formal commander.

In the retinue of the Emperor of Russia: **General Quartermaster** Sukhtelen; **General Inspector of Artillery** Count GL Araktchejev, Adjutants: GL Prince Dolgoruki (who on the day of battle commanded the Bagration infantry), GM Count Liven, GM Prince Gagarin, GM Prince Volkonski, GM Baron Wintzingerode; GM Intzov, General of the Day.

Following H.M. **Imperial Franz I**: FML Prince Schwarzenberg, FML Lambert, aide de camp of the emperor

1st Regiment Austrian cuirassiers Kaiser Franz (2 sq. - 141) assigned to the defense of the General Staff

Austrian Army Commander Prince Johann Liechtenstein.

The Russian Chief of Staff Major Gerhard Franz von Weyrother CdSM Austrian, assisted by GM Bubna.

Russian Imperial Guard Grand Duke Constantin

1st Column of the Guard Grand Duke Constantin

Grenadiers Preobrazhenski 2 btg (I and III) 1491 Shef Emperor Aleksandr I - com. GL Piotr Aleksandrovich Count Tolstoi - field comm. PK Mikail Timofejovich Kozlovsky

Grenadiers Semenovski 2 btg (I and III) 1487 - Shef Emperor Aleksandr I - com. GM Leontii Ivanovich Depreradovich-I

Izmailovski Grenadiers 2 btg (I and III) 1461 Shef Grand Duke Nikolai Pavlovich - com. GL Piotr Fiodorovich Maliutin - field comm. PK Matvjei Evgrafovich Khrapovitski.

Jäger of the Guard (Leib-Gvard Eger)1 btg 483 - Shef GL Piotr Ivanovich Bagration - com. PK Emmanuel Frantsevich Sen Pri (Saint-Prix)

Cuirassiers of the Guard (Leib-Gvard) 5 sq. 784 - Shef Grand Duke Constantin Pavlovich - com. GM Ivan Fiodorovich Yankovich

Hussars of the Guard (Leib-Gvard Gusaren) 5 sq 690, Shef Gen. Cav.Grand Duke Liudvig Viurtembergsky (Württemberg)- com. GL Andrei Simionovich Kologrivov

Artillery Battalion of the Guard (Leib-Gvard) GM Ivan Fiodorovich Kaspersky - Ca-vallo Artillery Company of the Guard 10 pieces, PK Vassili Grigorjevich Kostenetski - Position Company of Btg. Guard artillery 12-piece PK Fiodor Fiodorovich Rall; Guard light artillery company 10-piece Captain Aleksandr Kristoforovich Eiler (148 u.) with 4 battalion guns for the Preobrazhenski; Guard light artillery company 10-piece PK Fiodor Ivanovich Resleyna (148 u) 8 battalion guns for the Sernenovski and Isrnailovski regiments. Eight guns from two light companies were unassigned and formed a combined battery (they were not used as battalion guns).

2nd Column of the Guard GL Piotr Fiodorovich Maliutin

Leib Gvard Grenadiers 3 btg, 2134 - Shef lmp. Aleksandr I - com. GL Vassili Mikailovich Lobanov

Cuirassiers of the Horse Guard 5 sq. - 766 - Shef GAd Fiodor Petrovich Uvarov, brigade commander in the V column - com. GM Nikolai Ivanovich Depreradovich-2

Leib-Gvard Cossacks 2 sq. 295, com. PK Piotr Abramovich Chernozubov-5

Artillery support position company of the 4th artillery regiment 6 pieces 121 u.; PK Aleksei Mertens

Light company of the Imperial Militia btg: 6 pieces (121 u.) These were probably battalion guns for the Leib-Gvard Gra-natiers.

In general, battalion guns were 6-pounder + 10-pounder Unicorns.

The artillery of the Horse Guard (light company) had 5 6-pounder cannons + 5 10-pounder Unicorns.

The heavy artillery of the Foot Guard had 4 medium 12 lb. cannons + 2 light 12 lb. cannons + 4 8 lb. unicorns.

Krenovice (Krenowitz): is the village where the two emperors retreated after abandoning the Pratzen. It is known only because, in that place, in the estate of Spáčil, Weyrother drew up his famous plan the night before the battle. According to the plan, the Allies were to descend against the French right, bypass it and strike on the flank in a northerly direction at Slatina. Around Krenovice on the Zlata Hora hill was one of the largest mass graves of the battle. In 2005, a monument was built in honor of Kutuzov, with his statue on the square in Křenovice. In addition, a com-memorative plaque, commemorating the Allied briefing, is located on the old Spáčil farm. In Krenovice you will also find the Church of St. Lawrence, where Russian prisoners were rounded up after the battle. In the village square, near the pastry shop and the lo-canda, you will also notice a curious parapet, close to the road, whose motif is formed by Napoleonic characters.

At the intersection of the roads from Prace to Křenovice and from Blažovice to Zbýšov there is a hump. In the moderately undulating landscape typical for South Moravia, this place is an ideal place for photos. A little further south is the monument to the three emperors.

Zbýšov (Sbischow): the Langeron column passed through Zbýšov on the eve of the battle to deploy on Pratzen. Liechtenstein's cavalry encamped further north, in the direction of Křenovice. Between 11 a.m. and 12 p.m. on December 2, 1805, the Russian and Austrian battalions retreated, under the protection of Liechtenstein's cavalry and Zocchi's artillery, through Zbýšov, Šaratice, and Křenovice to Slavkov. There are two memorials of the battle here: the chapel of Our Lady of Sorrow in the village square has some cannonballs in the wall. Northeast of the village is a cross built over a mass grave. The bones were moved to Krchůvek near Křenovice and the cross itself today is no longer in its original location.

▲ Peace Monument on the Pratzen

Mohyla míru (Peace Monument - Pratzen): accessed via a road full of hairpin bends and is a vantage point for the southern side of the battle. Napoleon and his Staff stopped at that location, near the chapel of St. Anthony of Újezd (Augezd), about 2 p.m. on December 2. They observed the end of the battle and the Allied retreat, tormented by French cannon fire, to the banks of the Satschan and Mönitz ponds. When the fire ceased, they descended into the valley. The monument is located on Pratzen Hill (Pratecký, 324 m), the highest point of the battle. In 1805, it was deforested and dominated the entire theater of the battle. Here stood the two Emperors, at the beginning of hostilities, with the territory garrisoned by the Kamenski column and the Kollowrath division. It will be occupied by the French of Saint-Hilaire, Thiebault, Varé and Levasseur at 11 am. The Austrian General Jurčik attempted an all-out defense, but the Austrian commander was wounded and died after the battle. This "Tumulus of Peace" was done in Art Nouveau style on the initiative of a Catholic priest, Father Alois Slovák, who insisted on forming a committee. It was designed by a Prague architect, Fantain in 1911. Later it also became the museum of the battle.

Facing Napoleon, on the hill near the village of Pratzen, was the center of the Austro-Russian deployment, with the headquarters of General Kutuzov, the Austrian Emperor Franz I, and Tsar Alexander I. On the Pratzen hill today stands the great monument to Peace (Mohyla míru) and an interesting museum of the battle.

The French Detachment of Kobelnitz, which belonged to Legrand's 3rd Division, defended the northern part of the southern sector, that of the frozen ponds. It was attacked by the 3rd Russian column.

2nd Brigade GdB Victor Levasseur

18th Line 2 btg 1507 - Col. Jean Baptiste Ambroise Ravier

75th line regiment 2 btg 1532 - Col. François L'Hullier

Corsican Light Battalion (Tirailleurs Corse) 1 btg 635 - Col. Philippe Antoine Ornano

3rd Russian Column GL lgnatii Yakovlevich Przbishevski

Vanguard GM Ivan Ivanovich Miller-III

7th Jäger Regiment (Eger) 2 btg. (I and II) 823 (battalion III was detached to I Column from 29 November) - Shef GM Ivan Ivanovich Miller-III (Müller) - com. PK Pavel Piotrovich Tolbukhin, who was in command of the I Column detachment

8th Jäger Regiment (Eger) 1 btg. (III) 286 detached from II Column on the morning of December 2 - com. PK Vassili Danilovich Laptjev, who commanded most of the regiment with the II Column.

Pioneer Company Virubov 160 men

Main body GM Fiodor Borisovich Strik

Regt. Musketeers Galitz or Halycz 3 btg. 1487 - Shef GM Ivan Antonovich Loshakov - com. PK Yakovlev Andrejevich Voeikov

Regt. Musketeers of Butyrsk 3 btg 2055 - Shef GM Fiodor Borisovich Strik, commander of the brigade - com. PPK Mikhail L'vovich Treskin

Regt. Musketeers of Narva 3 btg 1921 - Shef GL Iosip Vasilievich Rotgof (perhaps absent) - com. ??

Artillery support 18 battalion guns

Reserve GL Georg Fridrik Baron Wimpfen

Regt. Musketeers of Podolsk 3 btg 799 - Shef GM Mikail Ivanovich Levitzkii - com. PPK Nechaev-II

Regiment Musketeers of Azov 3 btg 996 - Shef GM Aleksei Abramovich Selekhov - com. PPK Otto Vladimirovich Shta-kel'berg

Supporting artillery: 12 battalion guns.

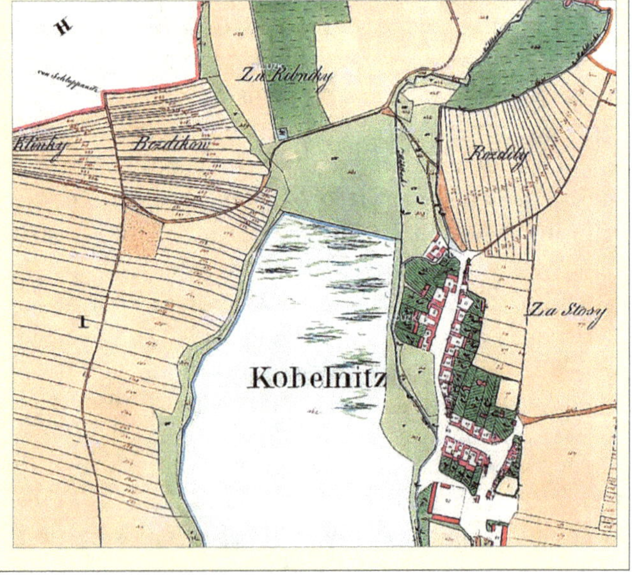

Kobylnice (Kobelnitz): Kobylnice, in 1805, was a village of a few houses. It was the site of numerous rearrangements of various French units. General Levasseur's right flank protected the right wing of the Saint-Hilaire division near Kobylnice during the attack on Pratzen, led by Soult. In the morning part of Oudinot's grenadier division came in support near the pheasantry, while the main part went against Przbishevski's troops. At the end of the battle the troops of Saint-Hilaire, Vandamme, and the Guard rotated south toward the Pratzen and surrounded Buxhöwden. Between 3 and 4 p.m., Przbishevski attempted to break out of the pocket to the north, but was repulsed by French grenadiers and then remained besieged in the village of Dvorska.

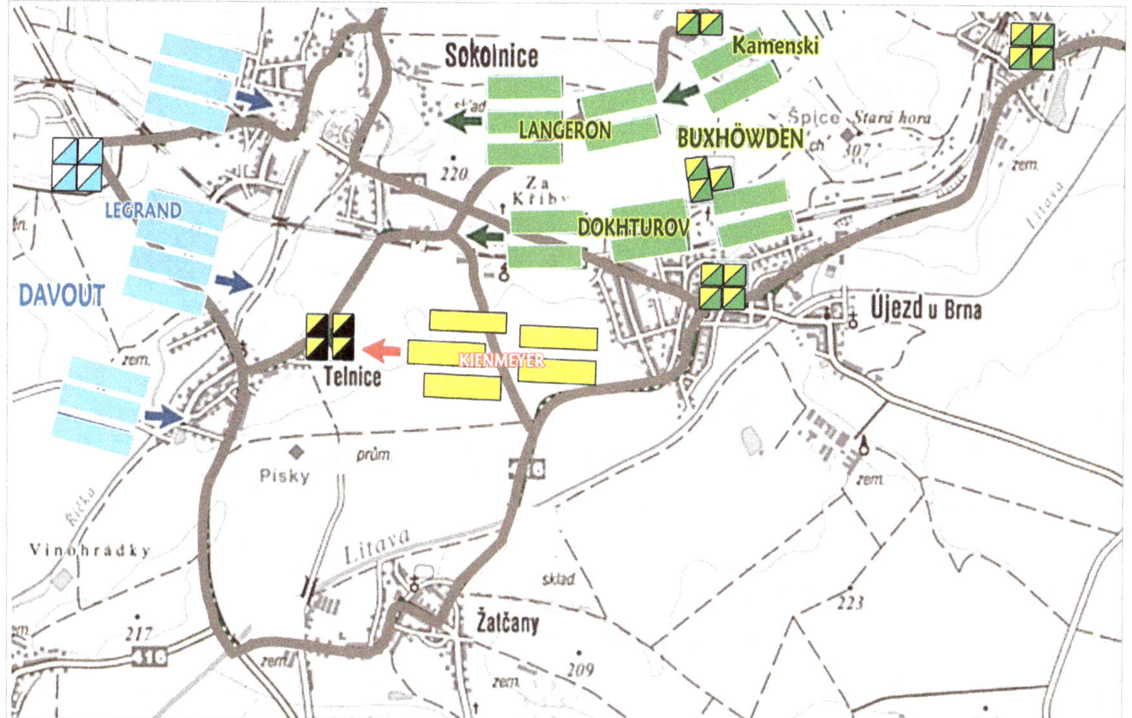

FRENCH RIGHT WING OR SOUTH SECTOR

The French right wing was deployed near the villages of Sokolnice (Sokolnitz) and Telnice (Telnitz), not far from the road from Brno to Vienna.

Sokolnice -Ujezd u Brna (Sokolnitz -Augezd) The southern sector of the battle. On the morning of December 2, the battle begins at Sokolnitz and Tellnitz. Allied columns of Dockhturov, Langeron, and Przbishevski attack the French right wing. The French battle strengthens, at 9 o'clock, with the arrival of Davout's corps from Rajhrad (Raygern) and Rebesovice (Rebeschowitz). The French engage in a flexible defense, preventing any breakthrough of the Allies. At 12 o'clock the French advance, behind the Allies, on Pratzen and the battle ends between 15 and 16 o'clock.

Sokolnitz is located on the right side of the Goldbach, eleven kilometers southeast of Brno. The first written mention of the village dates back to 1408. The Dietrichstein and Mittrovsky princely dynasties are intimately linked to its history for having owned Sokolnice Castle for several generations. It was originally a Renaissance fortress that the Dietrichsteins bought in 1705 for 154000 forints. The domain of Sokolnice consisted of six villages - Horákov, Ko-belnice, Ponětovice, Sokolnice, Telnice and part of Jiříkovice. In the middle of the 18th century the old fort was reconstructed as a one-story castle with three wings by the Baroque architect Antonín Grim, who remade it in the French style. Sokolnitz Castle, with its clock tower crowned by a Latin cross, was nevertheless a quite extraordinary building in Moravia. Its last noble owners were the Mittrovsky family from Nemyšle, who gave the castle its present neo-Gothic appearance after it was burned down during the battle in 1843. Today it houses a home for pensioners. Sokolnitz, with its central building (castle), palace, granary and pheasantry was the center of the French southern defense. Here the Legrand and Friant divisions held out against as many as three Allied columns (I-II-III of Generals Dokhturov, Langeron and Przbishevski. After the battle the granary, a monumental baroque building, was used as a prison for about 400 Russians; behind the building the prisoners buried the fallen in a mass grave.

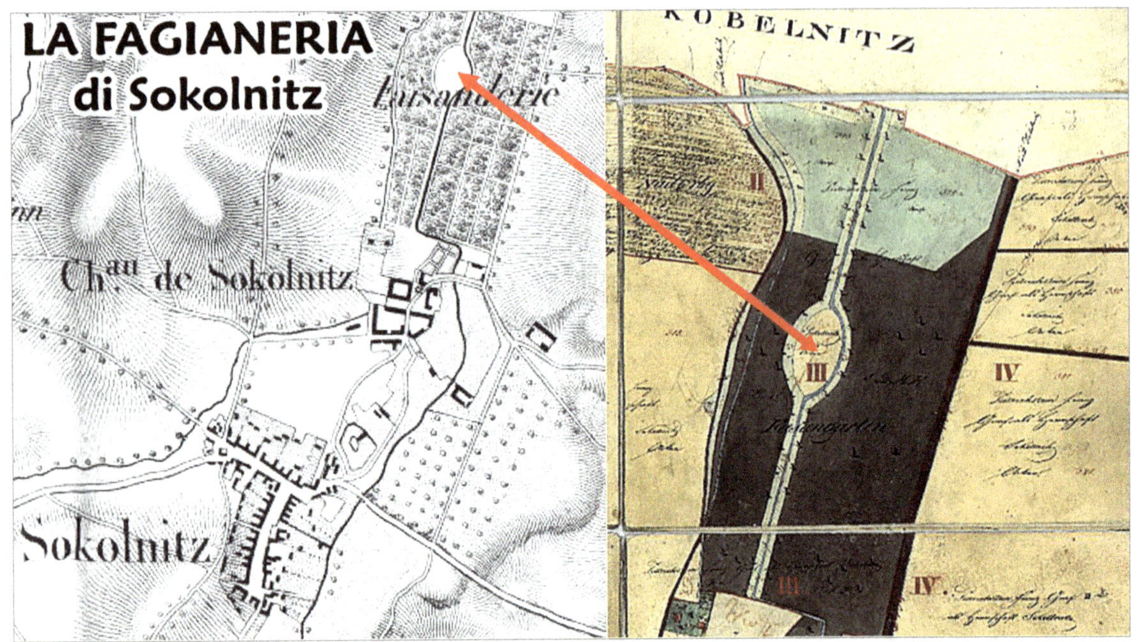

Sokolnitz the Pheasantry - The beautiful castle park is open to the public, along with its hunting grounds (the Pheasantry), where the Golbach River passes through, and where rare plants are found. The castle chapel, dedicated to the Elevation of the Holy Cross, can be visited on request. It was consecrated in 1750. The battle of Austerlitz is commemorated by a French cast-iron grenade that was built into the wall of the castle's old forest house. The Pheasantry, which is located nearby, or rather the wall surrounding the park, is the subject of lively debate among historians. There are doubts about the authenticity of the firing position of the five French cannons. The age of the perimeter wall is also disputed - from some sources it appears to have been erected in the second half of the 19th century (so it was not there during the battle of Austerlitz). Five crosses or marks on the perimeter wall of the pheasantry, on the side facing Kobelnitz, mark the location of five French pieces. There are no reliable sources to prove that the French had placed cannons in those spots. Moreover, given the wall, the cannons would have had to fire upwards, a useless, and disadvantageous, thing if the enemy had occupied the hill in front of the Pheasantry. On the other hand, it is unthinkable that the French could have faced two Russian columns without artillery.

3rd Division GdD Claude Juste Alexandre Legrand
1st Brigade GdB Pierre Hugues Victoire Merle
26th Light Regiment 2 btg 1587 - Col. François René Pouget
3rd Brigade GdB Jean Baptiste Michel Féry
Light Battalion «Tirailleurs du Po» 1 btg 587 - Col. Etienne Hulot
3rd Line Regiment 3 btg 1888 - Col. Laurent Schobert
Artillery - 14th company of 5th regiment 8 pieces (2 8-pounders + 2 4-pounders + 2 6-inch howitzers) (+ 2 8-pounders - detachment of 16th company of 5th regiment) - 213 u.
Light Cavalry Brigade GdB Pierre Margaron
11th Regiment. Chasseurs à cheval 3 sq. 317 - Col. Bertrand Bessières
26th Regt. Chasseurs à cheval 3 sq. 331 - Col. Alexandre Elisabeth Michel Digeon
Detachment of the 8th regiment, Hussars 3 sq. 276 - Col. Jean Baptiste Francheschi-Delosne
4th company of 5th regiment on horseback - 5 8-pounder pieces - 143 u.

Corps Artillery

17th and 18th comp. of the 5th Mounted Regiment 6 pieces of 8 lbs., 250 u. - Chef-de-Brigade Fontenoy

III Corp Maréchal Louis Nicolas Davout

2nd Division GdD Louis Friant

Brigade Vanguard GdB Etienne Heudelet de Bierre

108th Line Regiment 2 btg. 818 - Col. Joseph Higonet

15th Light Regiment 63 u. in 2 companies

1st Brigade GdB Georges Kister

15th Light Regiment 2 bt. 754 - Maj. Jean Michel Geither

33rd Line Regiment 2 btg. 607 - Col. Jean Saint-Raymond.

2nd Brigade GdB Pierre Charles Lochet

48th Line 2 btg. 633 - Col. Joseph Barbanegre

111th Line Regiment 2 btg. 720 - Col. Jacques François Gay

Artillery 2nd Comp. of 7th regiment on foot 6 pieces (4 8-pounder cannons + 2 howitzers) - 1st Comp. of 5th regiment on horseback 3 pieces (2 8-pounder cannons and 1 howitzer) - 286 u.

1st Cavalry Reg. Dragoons 3 sq. 329 - Col. Jean Thomas Arrighi de Casanova (detached from 1st Div. Dragoons)

4th Division Dragoon François Antoine Louis Bourcier

1st Brigade GdB Jean Baptiste Antoine Laplanche

15th Regiment Dragoons 3 sq. 338 - Col. Nicolas Martin Barthélémy

17th Regiment Dragoons 3 sq. 364 - Col. Joseph Nicolas de St Dizier

27th Regt. Dragoons 3 Sq. 347 - Col. Denis Teyrere

2nd Brigade GdB Louis Michel Sahuc

18th Regiment Dragoons 3 Sq. 334 - Col. Charles Lefebvre-Desnouettes

19th Regt. Dragoons 3 Sq. 412 - Col. Auguste Jean Gabriel Caulaincourt

Artillery 3rd Comp. of 2nd Regt. Mounted 3 pieces (2 8-pounder guns and one howitzer) 88 u.

Telnice (Tellnitz, near the road): not far from a railway underpass, along the road between Sokolnice and Tel-nice, was the tip of the French right wing, protected by the bank of a stream, then called the "Goldbach" or Zlatý potok. Davout deployed his troops, who had left Vienna on the 29th, directly on the march. According to Napoleon's orders they were to make a flexible defense, retreating when necessary to avoid encirclement. Here, on the banks of the Goldbach, the Legrand and Bourcier cavalry divisions also fought against the Austrian FML Kienmayer and the Russian generals Dokhturov and Langeron.

In the northern part of Telnitz there is a neighborhood called "Na lopatě" (above the shovels). Here there was a violent skirmish between the Austrian Hussar captain Lažanský and French tirailleurs.

Left Wing GL Fiodor Fiodorovich Buxhöwden

The commander of the Allied left wing or the first three columns (the Russians pronounced him Buksghevden)

2nd Russian Column GL Alexander Andrault de Langeron

Vanguard PK Vassili Danilovich Laptev

8th Jäger Regiment (Eger) 2 btg. (I and II) 572. The 3rd btg. had been detached to the 3rd column at 9 a.m. on December 2 - com. PK Vassili Danilovich Laptev

Pioneer Company Berg 160 u.

Main Corps GM Zakhar Dmitrievich Olsufiev-III

Regt. Musketeers of Vyborg 3 btg. 2052 - Shef GM Zakhar Dmitrievich Olsufiev-III, brigade commander - com. PPK Egor Maksimovich Pillar

Regt. Perm Musketeers 3 btg. 2047 - Shef GL Georg Fridrik Baron Wimpfen, commander a brigade of the 3rd column - com. PK Andrei Andrejevich Kuznetsov

Regt. Musketeers of Kursk 3 btg. 2032 - Shef GL Ignatii Yakovlevich Przbishevski, commander of the 3rd column - com. PK Aleksei Matvjejevich Seleventov

Supporting artillery: 18 battalion guns (6-pounders or 10-pounders unicorns).

Reserve Brigade GM Sergei Mikailovich Kamenski-I

Regt. Musketeers of Ryazan 3 btg. 2054 - Shef GL Aleksei Fedorovich Lanzheron or "Langeron" commander of the 2nd co-colony - com. PPK Bogdanov

Regt. Musketeers of Fanagoria 3 btg. 2042 - Shef GM Sergjei Mikailovich Kamenski-I brigade commander - com. ??

Support artillery 12 battalion guns (6-pounders or 10-pounders Unicorns)

Supporting cavalry PPK Mikail Dmitriyevich Balk detached from the 5th column on the morning of 2 December

Regiment St. Petersburg Dragoons 2 sq. IV and V sq. (part of 5th column)

Regiment Cossacks Issaiev 1 sq. (part of the 5th column)

Hostěrádky-Rešov (Hostieradek - Reschow) Practically two independent villages on the slope of the Old Hill (Stará hora). Nearby were deployed soldiers of Dokhturov's vanguard, facing Sokolnice and Kobylnice. General Kienmayer's Austrian column, formed by Grenzer, was further south. Russian General Langeron was deployed on the northwest slope. After 7 a.m. Dokhturov left Pratzen to descend on Hostieradek and Augezd, toward Tellnitz.

▲ Map of the battle from reconnaissance

> **The Chapel of St. Anthony.** Shortly after noon, the French occupied the Pratzen Plateau and fighting ceased in the central sector of the battlefield. Napoleon's divisions began to advance toward the southwest. Napoleon himself met the Staff of Marshal Soult at the chapel of St. Anthony of Padua, on the hill above Augezd (Újezd u Brna). From there he observed the withdrawal of the Allied troops in the afternoon. He was so pleased with the outcome of the triumphant end of the battle that he embraced Marshal Soult, something quite extraordinary for Napoleon.

▲ The area of frozen ponds

1st Russian Column GL Dmitrii Sergjejevich Dokhturov-I

Vanguard GM Ivan Ivanovich Miller-III

7th Jäger Regiment (Eger) 1 btg. (III) 413 detached from the 3rd column on 29 November - Shef GM Ivan Ivanovich Miller-III co-commanding the brigade of the 3rd column - com. PK Pavel Piotrovich Tolbukhin

5th Jäger Regiment (Eger) 1 btg. (III) 396 3rd Battalion. Btg. I and II were detached to the vanguard of Bagration from 29 November - Shef PK Fiodor Grigorjevich Gogel - com. Maj. Fiodor Ivanovich Pantenius commander of the main body of the regiment

Pioneer Company Kudzevich 160 u.

Brigade GM Fiodor Fiodorovich Leviz

Regg. Musketeers of Novoingermanland 3 btg. 1787 - Shef and com. GL lvan Karlovich Baron Rozen

Regiment Musketeers of Yaroslav 3 btg. 1337 - Shef GM Fiodor Fiodorovich Leviz (Löwis) brigade commander - com. PPK Osip Karlovich Sokolovsky

Supporting artillery: 12 battalion guns.

Brigade GM Nikolai Ivanovich Liders

Regt. Musketeers of Vladimir 3 btg. 1543 - Shef GM Sergjei Kornilovich Shevliakov - com. PPK Timofei Ivanovich Zbievsky

Regt. Musketeers of Bryansk 3 btg. 1311 - Shef GM Nikolai Ivanovich Liders, commander of the brigade - com. PPK Nikolai Kirillovich Rubanov-I

Supporting artillery: 12 battalion guns.

Brigade GM Nikolai Iurévich prince Urusov-l

Regt. Musketeers of Vyatka 3 btg. 1289 - Shef GM Nikolai Iurévich Prince Urusov-I, commander of the brigade - com. PK Bibikov

Regt. Musketeers of Moscow 3 btg. 1637 - Shef GL Dmitrii Sergjejevich Dokhturov, commander of the 1st column - com. PK Nikolai Simionovich Sulima

Regg. Kiev Grenadiers 3 btg. 1172 - Shef GL Karl Fridrik prince Saksen-Veimarsky (Sachsen-Weimar) "Honorary" - com. GM Ivan Nikitich Inzov, Day General

Artillery support 16 battalion guns

Heavy artillery PK Count Yakov Karlovich Sivers - Position battery of the 3rd artillery regiment 12 pieces, 250 u. - PK Count Sivers - Position battery of the 3rd artillery regiment 12 pieces, 250 u. - Major Sigizmund

Support cavalry - Don Cossacks Regiment Denissov 2 sq. 200.

Austrian Left Vanguard FML Michael Baron von Kienmayer

Cavalry Brigade GM Johann Nepomuk Nostitz

4th Regiment Hussars Hessen-Homburg 6 sq. 225 - Oberst Johann Freiherr von Mohr

2nd Regt. Ulani Schwarzenberg - half sq. 100 from regimental depot

1st Regt. Ulani Merveldt half sq. 40 from regimental depot

Cavalry Brigade GM Moritz Baron Liechtenstein

11th Regiment Székler Hussars 5 sq. 500 - Oberst Gabriel Geringer von Oedenburg

Cavalry Brigade GM Karl Baron von Stutterheim

3° O'Reilly cavalry regiment 8 sq. 900 - Oberst Friedrich Count Degenfeld-Schonburg

Artillery support Austrian horse battery 4 pieces 125 u. - Oberst Degenfeld

Infantry Brigade GM Carneville

15th Regt. Grenzer or II Székler 2 btg 1100 - Oberst Johann Chevalier Grammont

14th Regt. Grenzer or I Székler 2 btg 1000 - Oberst Georg Ritter von Knesevich died of wounds sustained at Austerlitz on 10 January 1806

7th Regt. Grenzer of Brod 1 btg. 500 - Oberstleutnant Desullenovich

Artillery support: 8 cannons of battalion
Detachment Oberstleutnant Rakovsky

Was unable to reach the column and merely covered the retreat of the 4th column

4th Regt. Hussars Hessen-Hornburg 2 sq. 75 - Oberstleutnant Rakovsky

11th Regt. Hussars Székler 1 sq. 100

Žatčany - Újezd (Satczan or Satschan- Augezd): the landscape below the southern slope of Pratzen passes south and southwest into a wide plain that, at the time of the battle, was covered by two large ponds - near the villages of Mönitz (Měnín) and Satschan (Žatčany). The former, with its 514 hectares, formed one of the largest aquifers in Moravia. After noon the Allies withdrew precipitously along the frozen ponds of Žatčany (Satschan) and Měnín (Mönitz), through Augezd in the direction of Austerlitz and Hodonín. Napoleon had a beautiful view, from the chapel of St. Anthony, in a southerly direction and could see well the three Russian columns in the valley, attacked on both sides by masses of French soldiers. In that area the Pratzen plateau changes (above Újezd) name to Stará hora (old mountain). In the afternoon the whole ridge of the plateau was invaded by thousands of French soldiers. Towards the end of the battle they made the same descent that the Allies had made in the morning. The latter found themselves stuck as if in a trap. From the northern sector of the plateau, masses of soldiers were approaching - Saint-Hilaire and Vandamme's division, Boyé's dragoon division, and six battalions of Oudinot's grenadiers.

In the front sector Davout, with the Friant division near Tellnitz and Sokolnitz, was pressing against the Russians, causing them to panic. The escape routes were quite narrow and the French attacked them from two directions. **Those who** had better luck and strength, opened a road to the south. But there was an unpleasant and complicated obstacle - both ponds.

The retreat of the Dokhturov column, along the frozen ponds, was plagued by French cannons now placed at the of the chapel of St. Anthony of Újezd. They said the shots cracked the ice and many sank into the frozen slime. Kienmayer's Border (Grenzer) troops, deployed along the Littawa valley, were protecting the retreat. Examination of the bottom of the ponds after the battle belied the hundreds of enemy deaths claimed by French sources. Nevertheless, the legend of the dead in the ponds ended up being fatal to the local fishery; thus the ponds were drained. The drained grounds became a favorable place for the cultivation of beet and wheat.

Augezd or Újezd u Brna is located 15 kilometers southeast of Brno and is one of the oldest villages in the region. Stone from the local quarry of the "old mountain" was used for the construction of the Peace Monument. The chapel of St. Anthony of Padua stands above the village. After the Battle of Austerlitz, the chapel's condition gradually deteriorated until 1841, when it was torn down. It was rebuilt 49 years later. The French historian and future president of the Third French Republic Louis Adolphe Thiers, who had personally visited Újezd, also wanted to participate in its re-building. Today you can also visit the place where Napoleon watched the end of the battle, despite the forests that obstruct a view.

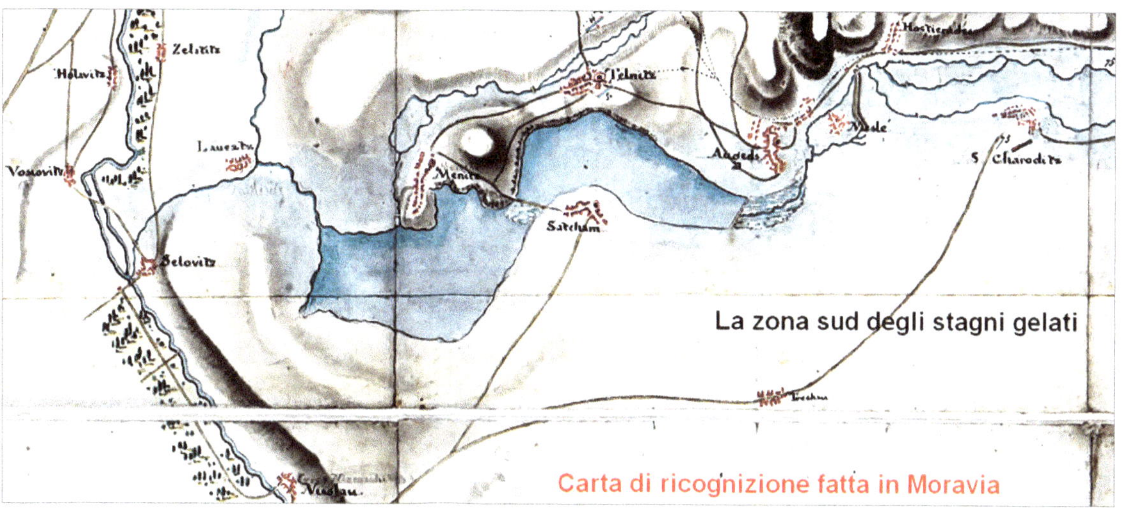

▲ General Kutusov, commander of the Allied troops, kneels in front of the sacred insignia.

▲ *The glory of Austerlitz*, by François Gérard.

PLATES

THE SOLDIERS OF AUSTERLITZ

FRANCE: PLATES BY NADIR DURAND

RUSSIA: PLATES BY A.V.VISKOVATOV

AUSTRIA: PLATES BY OTTENFELD

▲ France Guard grenadier and infantryman.

▲ France line artilleryman and horse artilleryman in the Guard.

▲ France hussars horse line.

▲ France armor and line dragons.

▲ Russia infantry with coat.

▲ Russia Guard Grenadiers.

▲ Russia cavalry dragoons.

▲ Russia cavalry cuirassiers.

▲ Austria infantry in combat.

▲ Austria line infantry.

▲ Austria Dragoons on horseback.

▲ Austria cuirassiers on horseback.

BIBLIOGRAPHY

Alombert, P. C. and J. Colin, *Campagne de 1805 en Allemagne, 5 Vols in 7*; Paris: Chapelot, 1902-8. *The revised edition includes a new 5th volume*

Austerlitz, Recits de soldats, Collection Épopée ed. da Robin Pierre d Christophe Dufourg Burg, Bernard Giovanangeli Editeur, 2006.

Béraud, Stéphane, *La revolution militaire napoleonienne, VOL. I « Les Manœuvres »*, Bernard Giovanangeli Editeur, 2007.

Béraud, Stéphane, *La revolution militaire napoleonienne, VOL. II « Les Batailles »*, Bernard Giovanangeli Editeur, 2015.

Bülow, Dietrich, *Die Feldzug von 1805 ; militärisch=politisch betrachtet*, vol. I, pubbl. in proprio, 1805.

Castle, Ian, *Austerlitz. Napoleon and the Eagles of Europe*, Pen & Sword Military 2018.

Colin, Jean, *La Campagne de 1805 en Allemagne*, Review d'Histoire, 1905-8.

Drouet d'Erlon, Jean-Baptiste, *Le Marechal Drouet, Comte d' Erlon : vie militaire*; Paris: G. Barba, 1844

Duffy, Christopher, *Austerlitz 1805*; London: Seeley Service, 1977

Garnier, Jacques, *Austerlitz 2 Decembre 1805*, Fayard 2005.

Goetz, Robert, 1805 Austerlitz - Napoleon and the Destruction of the Third Coalition, Greenhill Books London 2005.

Hanak, Jaromìr, *Guide to the Area of the Battle of Three Emperors*, Ave Brno 2015.

Kriegs Archiv, Wien, *Kriege unter der Regierung des Kaisers Franz: Krieg gegen die französische Revolution*, 2 vols. (Vienna, 1905).

La Moravie de Napoléon, in < https://www.morava-napoleonska.cz/fr/ >.

Langeron, Alexandre Andrault de, *Journal Inedit de la Campagne de 1805: Austerlitz*, With Karl Freiherr von Stutterheim, Mikhail Hilairionovich Golenistchev-Kutusov, Relations de la Bataille d'Austerlitz; Paris: La Vouivre, 1998.

Larrey, Dominique-Jean, *Mémoires de Chirurgie Militaire et Campagnes*, 4 vol., Paris, 1812-1817.

Mayerhoffer von Vedropolje, Eberhard, *1805, Der Krieg der 3. Koalition gegen Frankreich*, Seidel u. Sohn, Vienna 1905.

Mikhailovski-Danilevski, A. (trad. dal ten. gen. Leon Narischkin), *Relation de la Campagne de 1805*; Paris: J. Dumaine, 1846.

Mikaberidze, Alexander, *The Russian Officer Corps in the Revolutionary and Napoleonic Wars, 1792-1815*; New York: Savas Beatie, 2005.

Moritz von Angeli, "Ulm und Austerlitz," in *Mitteilungen des k.u.k. Kriegs Archivs*, III (1878): 283-394

Podmazo, Aleksandr, „*Shefy I Komandiry Regularnykh Polkov Russkoi Armii, 1796-1815*“; <http://www.museum.ru/museum/1812/Library/Podmazo/>

Rüstow, Wilhelm, *Der krieg von 1805 in Deutschland und Italien*; Frauenfeld: Verlags-Comptoir, 1853.

Six, Georges, *Dictionnaire Biographique des Generaux et Amiraux Français de la Revolution et de l'Empire (1792-1814)*, 2 Vols; Paris: Gaston Saffroy, 1934; facsimile reprint 1974

Sokolov, Oleg, *Austerlitz, Napoléon, l'Europe et la Russie*, Commios, 2006.

Souvenirs de guerre du Général Baron Pouget, pubblicato da Mme de Boideffre nata Pouget, Paris, Librairie Plon, 1895.

Stutterheim, Major-General [Karl], *A Detailed Account of the Battle of Austerlitz*; Cambridge: Ken Trotman, 1985.

Thiébault, Paul Charles François, *Mémoires du Général Baron Thiébault*, 5 vol. Paris, Plon 1893-95.

Uhlíř Dušan, *Bitva Tří císařů, Slavkov/Austerlitz 1805*, Ave Brno 1999.

Vanicek, Frantisek, *Specialgeschichte der Militärgrenze, aus Originalquellen und Quellenwerken geschopft*; 4 vol., Vienna: Kaiserlich-Koniglichen Hof- und Staatsdruckerei, 1875.

Vasil'ev, A., „*Russkaya Gvardiya v srazhenii Pri Austerlitse, 20 Noyabrya (2 Dekabrya) 1805 g.*" Voin Nos 3 &. 4; <http://www.genstab.ru/voin/auster 0 l .htm>.

Viskovatov, *Istoricheskoe Obozrenie Leib-Gvardii Izmailovskago Polka, 1730-1850* GG; St Petersburg: 1850.

Viskovatov, A. V. (traduzione di Mark Conrad), *Historical Description of the Clothing and Arms of the Russian Army: Volume 1 Oa, Organization 1801-1825*; Hopewell, NJ: On Military Matters, 1993. testo originale russo at <http://www.museum.ru/museum/1812/Army/Viskowatov/index.html>. St Petersburg, 1851

Wagner, Walter, *Von Austerlitz bis Königgrätz, Österreichische Kampftaktik im Spiegel der Reglements 1805 – 1864*, Studien zur Militärgeschischte, Militärwissenschaft und Konfliktforschung, Biblio Verlag, Osnabrück 1978.

Wrede, Alphons, *Geschichte der K. und K. Wehrmacht*, Vols 1-6; Vienna: L. W Seidel &. Sohn, 1898-1901.

▲ Knights of the Russian Guard under the command of Repnin, during a clash at the Battle of Austerlitz.

CONTENTS

▲ Memorial Tomb of Generalmajor Franz Jurczik (1758-1805) commanded in battle a brigade of inexperienced recruits, Austrian, Czech and Moravian soldiers who stopped in front of a French infantry of veterans showing courage in wanting to defend the Pratzen. The general was seriously wounded in the battle dying in the hospital about two weeks later.

TITOLI PUBBLICATI - ALREADY PUBLISHING

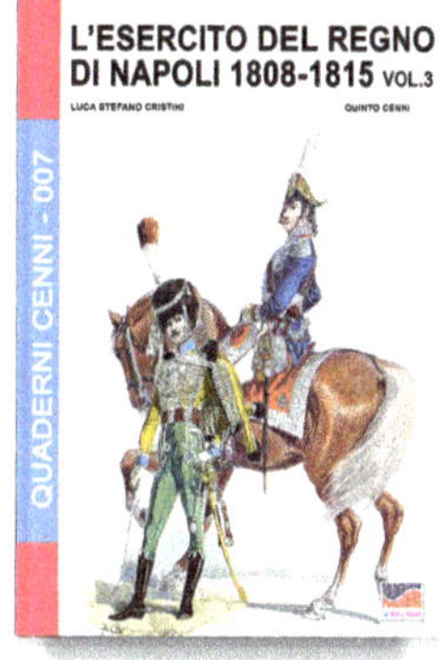

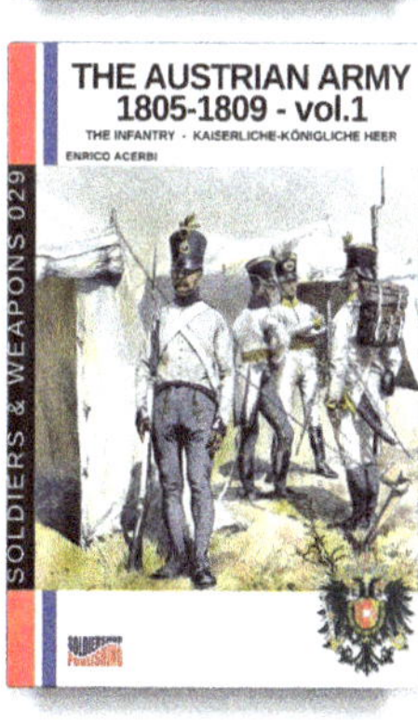

BATTLEFIELD 027